What readers are saying about
Arthur: The dog who crossed the jungle to find a home . . .

'Such a lovely story. I read it in one sitting with tears streaming down my face.' *****

'This book is just un-putdownable! For any dog lover it is a must-read and brings a tear to the eye.' *****

'An amazing and heart-warming book' *****

'You can't help but be moved by this wonderful partnership whether you are a dog lover or not' *****

'Amazing book, has made me smile, cry and kept me on edge of my seat. A truly touching true story about the bond of man and dog. A must-read.' *****

'Absolutely in love with this book!' *****

'I could not put this book down, had happy tears streaming down my face through the majority of the book' *****

'One of the best books I have read i

'Wonderful book and wonderful do
book over and over again' *****

800 701 483

'A truly heart-warming story of love and compassion between a man and a wonderfully courageous dog' *****

'Made me smile and made me cry. Fabulous book.' *****

'Absolutely amazing story, very moving' *****

'Oh how I loved this book, I read it in a day!' *****

'The most amazing story of love and devotion and a powerful story of kindness. Thank you for sharing this uplifting story with the world. We need it.' *****

'What a story! Books never make me cry – until I read this one.' *****

'A heart-warming tale that will leave you wanting more' *****

'Arthur is a dog in a million' *****

'This is not just a story of a dog being rescued, this is a story of a wonderful friendship between a man and a dog that grew in exceptional circumstances' *****

'Brilliant, gripping from the first page to the last' *****

'An amazing story of love and tenacity and a must for any dog lover – it is a classic in the making' *****

Arthur and Friends

Also by Mikael Lindnord and Val Hudson

Arthur: The dog who crossed the jungle to find a home

Arthur and Friends

*The further adventures of the
rescue dog from the jungle*

MIKAEL LINDNORD

With Val Hudson

TWO
ROADS

www.tworoadsbooks.com

First published in Great Britain in 2017 by Two Roads
An imprint of John Murray Press
An Hachette UK company

First published in paperback in 2018

1

Paperback ISBN 978 1 473 66164 6
Ebook ISBN 978 1 473 66165 3

Typeset in Cochin by Hewer Text UK Ltd, Edinburgh
The picture credits on page 203 constitute an extension of this copyright page
Printed and bound by CPI Group (UK) Ltd, Croydon, CR0 4YY

Hodder & Stoughton policy is to use papers that are natural, renewable
and recyclable products and made from wood grown in sustainable
forests. The logging and manufacturing processes are expected to
conform to the environmental regulations of the country of origin.

Hodder & Stoughton Ltd
Carmelite House
50 Victoria Embankment
London EC4Y 0DZ

www.hodder.co.uk

For Arthur, my best friend for life

Contents

Foreword

From the moment I noticed a tired and hungry dog quietly begging for food in a dusty Ecuadorian village three years ago, my life changed. It changed for the better, and it changed in ways I had never imagined or expected.

The fact that Arthur is now living happily with us as a much-loved member of our family back in Sweden is in huge part due to the groundswell of support I had from people all over the world. People who wanted

Arthur to be safe, and for us to live happily ever after – together. Ever since that fateful day and the struggles to save him, those people ask me – on a daily basis – how he is, how he's getting on, how we are all getting on.

I love talking about my friend (because he *is* my friend) Arthur, so I was only too happy to succumb to the pleas from everyone to tell the story of what has happened since our first book. In the course of writing, I couldn't help reliving some of those struggles in the Ecuadorian jungle, so I have written about them a little as well. I hope everyone will bear with me and Arthur in the retelling of the old, as well as enjoy the story of the new.

I also hoped that the story of Arthur's rescue, and his new life being happy and loved, would strike a chord with all those who are thinking of helping rescue dogs, or who just love dogs. In the event I was amazed by how many

people got in touch to tell me their own stories of rescue dogs around the world, dogs who had somehow found their person and made a life together. I hope their stories will be an inspiration too.

Mikael Lindnord, autumn 2017

Chapter One

Deep in the Heart of the Jungle

'Go the extra mile; it's never crowded there'

The jungle, Ecuador, November 2014

The vegetation was getting even more impenetrable, and more and more mud was sticking to our boots with every step we took. All four of our team were probably as exhausted as we had ever been, and in this business of extreme racing that is an exhaustion that most people can't really begin to imagine.

I looked down at the new fifth member of our team: a filthy, wounded dog, covered in mud and blood. As he trod slowly through the swampy earth, dragging each paw out of the ground with a visible effort, you could see that somewhere underneath the matted fur was a beautiful golden creature. As we struggled on, side by side, I found myself unconsciously matching him step for step. Not wanting to get ahead of him, because he was clearly finding it so hard to keep up, and yet not wanting to slow down to the point where we had no hope of staying in this increasingly gruelling race.

The Adventure Racing World Championship was – is – the pinnacle of the year for adventure racers. And this race, in the heart of the Ecuadorian jungle, was the climax of months and months of heart-bursting, leg-busting training. Staffan, Karen, Simon and I had set out as a team of four highly trained athletes determined to come in the top three of the adventure racing world, if not in the top one. And yet now, as the captain of our highly trained team, I found myself distracted and preoccupied by the struggling dog by my side.

He seemed to ask for no pity; he just seemed to be quietly determined not to leave my side. All I had done was notice him, talk to him and give him some food. And yet in the intense, feverish atmosphere of the jungle, I felt myself drawn to this struggling creature as he appeared to be drawn to me.

At one point he suddenly disappeared; shot off into the vegetation in search of some creature that only he could see or smell. I told myself that he was probably gone for ever,

on some mission that a mere human couldn't understand, and that I had just been imagining that there was some kind of bond between us. I bit my lip at the thought of never seeing him again. I couldn't believe that a dog – random, stray, appearing out of nowhere – could have so affected me.

And then, almost as quickly as he'd gone, he was back. Looking unblinkingly at the path ahead, walking determinedly by my side as if he'd never left it.

Perhaps that was the moment when I knew for certain that this dog and I would always be walking side by side.

Örnsköldsvik, November 2015

Bike gloves – check; mosquito nets – check; trekking boots – check. As I laid out all my kit in the sitting room ready for the journey to Brazil and the next championship race, I thought about how this time last year I was making the

3

same familiar preparations for Ecuador. Then I had had the help of Helena, and the occasional distraction from little Philippa, but now the house was full of noise and activity as three-month-old Thor made his presence felt from around the corner in the kitchen.

By my feet was the quiet presence of the other new member of the family, the now sleekly golden Arthur. He was lying on his shiny black bed, one paw tucked under him in his usual position, and looking calmly up at me as I laid my kit out, as if to say, 'I know what you're doing. And it means you're going away. But I know you're coming back. I trust you to come back.'

I put down the kitbag that I had been filling with head-lamps and batteries and went over to Arthur. I knew he trusted me, but I somehow felt I needed to take a moment to reassure him.

'Hey, boy,' I said as I knelt down in front of him. 'You know I'm coming back, don't you?' I scratched his dark gold ears and put my nose an inch away from his. Arthur's gaze – his amber eyes ringed by the distinctive black lines that seemed to emphasise his air of wisdom and calm – was unwavering.

I gave him a quick kiss on the tip of his nose and turned to pick up my son. Thor was waving his arms at Arthur, so I held him nearer so he could say hello. Once he was close enough, he put out his tiny chubby hand and gave Arthur's nose a friendly squeeze.

Arthur, the most regal and gentlemanly of dogs, remained calm and gentle as ever, just as he had done from the very first moment he had met the newborn Thor. He just lowered his head onto his paw, looked up at us, from one to the other, gave a small sigh and shut his eyes.

For all that the preparations were so familiar, it was strange, this year, to be leaving behind a family of four.

It was almost a year to the day since I had first met Arthur, but it was as if he had always been a part of us. In fact, it's hard for me – and Helena – to remember a time before Arthur, hard to imagine that we ever planned a day without thinking about how he would fit in.

People often ask me how he's changed us, how we managed to suddenly accommodate a dog into our lives. I only have one answer: he is just part of the family, no more and no less.

The jungle, Brazil, November 2015

The championship in Brazil was always going to be a major challenge and a hugely important race for us as a team. We were on track to keep our place in the top five in the world if we did as well as we hoped we would and finished in the top six. We knew we could do it and had, as ever, done months of training and preparation for this highlight of the year. Just as we had on the way out to Ecuador, we had checked and double-checked our kit and our strategies, and were fresh and fit from weeks of intense training – both at home and in camp in Turkey.

The people who designed the championship course in Brazil had announced that the race in the Pantanal wetlands of western Brazil would be very challenging and absolutely unforgettable. They were dead right on both counts.

I have been to any number of dangerous, uncomfortable places in the course of my adventure racing career, but this place probably beat all records. We were told to expect jaguars, wild boar, crocodiles and snakes, not to mention bullet ants, tarantulas and tropical mosquitoes. It was as close to Indiana Jones as you could possibly get.

And in addition, the organisers had no regulations about when to sleep or rest; there were no 'dark zones' – it was just first past the finish post. The maps had only the sketchiest of details, the terrain was as swampy, dense and unmanageable as we'd ever encountered, and all this in temperatures of over 40 degrees.

We were a different team from the one in Ecuador; Staffan and I were this year joined by Marika and Jonas. We were a well-knit team, though, and I was pleased that we'd come second in the Chile series in the summer. It would be a tough race but we were ready for it, I thought.

One of the members of one of the other teams had spent the morning before the start of the race talking and reading with a class of small children. They asked her if she was afraid of jaguars. When she asked them if she should be, they all nodded long and seriously. It turned out that all of them had already met a jaguar. I wasn't sure whether to be encouraged that they'd all survived the experience, or worried that we wouldn't.

The beginning of the race was a paddle up the river. That was only as nice as it sounds for about an hour or so. Soon the heat was intense, one of our boats leaked and we were attacked by clouds of man-eating mosquitoes. The wait for a new boat wasted valuable time, so at the next trekking stage we tried to push through the vegetation as fast as we could. Perhaps too fast, but we were still fresh enough to keep up a good pace, running along the trail whenever we could.

Head down and concentrating on the track, I half registered the signs of jungle creatures that had been that way before us. Then, as I focused more intently on the ground, I noticed a series of huge paw prints. The noise of our progress meant that at first I didn't hear the sinister sounds of rustling a couple of metres to my right. At that point I was slightly ahead of the others, so I paused to check that it wasn't just my imagination. No – there was another rustle and, I could swear, the sound of chewing. To be able to hear such a thing so loudly, I could only assume it was a creature big enough to match the paw prints. A huge cat. A jaguar.

I felt every muscle in my body tense as I remembered pictures I'd seen of jaguars in full hunting mode. But then I found myself thinking of Arthur, the world's most enthusiastic chaser of cats. What would he have done if he were here? Did I smell of dog, and was that a good thing or a bad thing? And then somehow, thinking of Arthur, with his aura of calm and his history of surviving in jungle as dangerous as this one, made me calm down. If he could survive in the jungle, then so could I.

I waited for the others and then, picking up speed, we headed downhill (always welcome, particularly in temperatures of 40 degrees) towards the 'transition area' and a large lake where we changed to pack-rafting. The others hadn't felt the presence of a jaguar, but Staffan assured me he had seen two wandering spiders, which the organisers' race notes had cheerfully assured us were generally considered to be 'the most venomous species of spider in the world'. Even aside from the sleep deprivation and exhaustion, adventure racing is not for the faint-hearted.

Pack-rafts are lighter and more stable than kayaks. They are also a lot slower. To start with we were on a network of rivers, so that didn't matter so much, but then, when we got out into the open onto another lake and facing a headwind, it mattered a lot. Progress was really slow and I was pretty sure we were now quite a way behind two of our major rivals – the Swedish Armed Forces team and the Lithuanians. So perhaps it was understandable that when we eventually made it to the landing area, the rest of the team were impatient to make swift progress up a steep hill rising out of the water.

I've been adventure racing for nearly twenty years, and I know that a cardinal rule when conditions are really extreme is to save your energy. So when you are in 40-degree heat and you have a practically vertical climb ahead of you, sprinting up it as fast as your legs will carry you is bound to lead to trouble. The thick jungle at the bottom was tough enough to get through, but the climb after that was hideous – hideously hot and hideously hard going.

I told the team to take it easy, we needed to conserve our strength. But just short of the summit there was a super-steep ridge, the last climb before the ground levelled off. From somewhere, Staffan got some kind of super-power and sped up on the last 50 metres. The rest of us sped up too to stay together but the burning heat – with no hint of a breeze – finally caught up with us, and we just sat there for a while, unable to move.

By the time we arrived at the next transition area, we were not in good shape – not helped by the fact that we'd run out of water. A section of the race that on the map had looked like a simple climb over a hill had been so much longer and tougher than we'd expected that we began to suspect that the whole race was going to be a whole lot harder than any we'd raced before.

The next stage started off with more heat and more hills, but then seemed not to have quite as many horrors as I'd imagined. We mostly walked along a boulder-strewn ridge where we could see over the plains of the Pantanal, and the gods gave us a breeze, which saved us from more direct hits from the infernal mosquitoes. Yet soon enough the sun reached its height and the intense heat returned, to make the second 35 kilometres as searingly exhausting as the previous day's climb. We'd run out of water again and this time the gods decided not to give us any creeks or rivers. We were desperately thirsty and, despite managing to get two or three hours' sleep in the relative cool of the night, seriously sleep-deprived.

I think thirst and heat makes everything worse, but in particular it makes you drained and very possibly stupid and muddle-headed. Certainly I found it hard to try to motivate everyone, and was depressed by the slow progress we seemed to be making. As a racing friend of mine says, 'When you're safe at home you wish you were adventure racing, and when you're racing you wish you were safe at home.' On an hourly basis my mind was taking me home.

By the time we got to the transition area we were all desperate for food, water and sleep. Especially sleep. But there wasn't time to rest properly; I needed everyone to be up and moving on – by my calculations we could gain at least two places if we cut short our rest.

So when we arrived at the waterside, ready for the kayaking leg, we were back in the sort of poor shape we'd been in the day before. Yet as I led the others down to the landing stage where the boats were waiting, I knew that we would have to make extra-good time on this leg to have any hope of regaining a top-five position.

As we got out the kayaks I could feel a light breeze at my back. We were going to be paddling downstream with a tailwind. For the first time in my racing life, we had ideal conditions for me to try out one of my race-winning theories. Tying the two boats together, I put up the small sail that lay buried deep in our equipment box. Marika and Staffan jumped into the first boat and Jonas and I climbed into the second one.

'Now we can get those two hours of sleep we need,' I said to the team as we pushed off. It worked like a dream. Roped together, we could take it in turns to paddle and sleep, navigating carefully in the dark and making good progress.

It wasn't a very comfortable sleep – wrapped in a light silver blanket, lying on the bottom of the kayak like pigs in blankets – but it meant we didn't need to sleep when we got to the next stage. And we got to the transition area more quickly than I could have hoped. It was one of the best stages in my racing career. So we set out on the next section – apparently the toughest of the race – in slightly better heart.

An hour later we were wading through swamp and rivers, making agonisingly slow progress. Everything in this particular jungle seemed to be either super-dry and bakingly hot, or swamps and water everywhere. There was nothing in between. This bit was a wet bit. And there was nothing for it but to wade through the water – poking our sticks ahead of us to check for stingrays – as best we could.

Another hour later and the stingrays were the least of our problems. There were some strange new creatures swimming round our legs. Remembering the organisers' helpful race notes, I realised what they were: piranhas – the kind of fish 'with a powerful bite that makes them adept at tearing flesh'.

'Whoa! This can't be happening,' I said to the others. 'But look at these guys. Piranhas. Seems like hundreds of them.'

'Okaaay,' said Jonas. 'Well, that's fine. I seem to remember it says in the book that they only attack if they're trapped, or if there's blood in the water.'

'Fine,' I said. 'Keep calm and don't bleed.'

I reckoned that was good advice for the next bit of the river too. We came round a bend just as it was starting to get dark, but I could make out lots of young crocodiles gathered on the bank. You could hear the snapping noises they made with their jaws. They sounded like they were revving up for a night of hunting.

As we waded slowly past them, through the swamp on the other side of the river, it was getting darker and darker. There was nothing for it but to turn our head-lamps on, even though we knew what would happen next.

Sure enough, as if waiting in the wings for lights, camera, action, out came the mosquitoes, the giant wasps and the flying ants. We could feel them biting us – vicious, irritating bites. It was getting harder and harder to keep calm and not bleed. Especially when we remembered that the Brazilians called this time of day, when it got dark, 'snake time'.

The last time we'd looked at the map it had been especially hard to check our position – reading a map on a scale of 1cm to 1km means there's not a lot of detail when you're somewhere in the middle of a 200,000-square-km jungle. I reckoned that we might well have been going in the wrong direction, but it was probably best to push on in the hope that we were heading roughly towards the right bit of water for the next stage.

'This is worse than Ecuador, isn't it? Only I suppose this time we haven't got a dog to worry about.' Staffan was bending over the map in frustration.

I felt a wave of weakness wash over me at the mention of Arthur. It suddenly hit me that here I was in this boiling heat on the other side of the world, and there he was back at home in the snow with the rest of our family. If I hadn't known how committed I was to this sport I would have wondered what I was doing here. For that moment, all I could do was stand still and take a moment to hope that he was enjoying a nice run in the snow and not missing me too much.

But meanwhile, the insects were increasing their attacks. To try to protect myself a bit I decided to turn off my headlamp and hope for the best. By this stage we'd run out of land; everywhere around us was water. So we started swimming, keeping in the same direction, with our poles in front of us to push off the thick vegetation and defend ourselves against the bigger snakes and fish.

We found land eventually and decided to rest up and check the map. Laying it on the ground, the four of us switched our lights on and bent over it. Just as our tired eyes focused on the bit of the map where we thought we were, we heard a piercing, terrifying series of loud squeals coming from our left. Wild boar. Herd of.

There was only water behind us, and jungle to our left and right. Staffan said he thought we should climb the three or four trees on the edge of the water. I thought they looked way too spindly to carry our weight, but the noise of screaming and hooves coming our way was now so loud that we would probably have tried climbing a piece of bamboo. Just as we started to pull ourselves up into the trees, there was another sound of screaming – coming from the opposite direction. Another herd of wild boar.

Somewhere in the jungle, they met in the middle. They must have come to some sort of agreement, because after another ear-splitting series of cries, the sound of hooves died away and we were left, shaken, by the edge of the river. In the quiet that followed, I suddenly heard a loud crunching noise. It was the sound of crocodile jaws snapping in the darkness nearby.

I thought it was probably OK to feel a little bit frightened.

It turned out that we had been going in the right direction, and it was only another three hours before we could see a landing strip and some buildings. When we slumped gratefully into the transition area we discovered that four teams had gone on, but the organisers had decided there wasn't going to be enough time to complete the course. With two days of race left there was still the pack-rafting leg to go, a 27-kilometre trek, 85 kilometres of kayaking and 251 kilometres of mountain biking. Even for highly trained endurance athletes that was going to be a tall order.

So the race was cut back and the waiting teams were airlifted out in three-seater planes to the final bike stage. Flying over the plains and jungles of the Pantanal, scrunched up in the tiny, noisy biplane, I wasn't in the mood to admire the view; instead I was busy working out the implications of all this for our position in the race. Although it was impossible to work out the rankings with any accuracy, I was pretty sure that if four teams were able to finish the race then our top six ranking overall for the year was in serious jeopardy. As we landed with teeth-shattering bumps on the rough landing strip, I felt pretty downbeat. Not a good mindset with which to go into the 250-kilometre biking leg – which had been billed as one of the toughest in an extremely tough race.

Almost as soon as we started, our bikes were slowed down to a crawl by the sand, which seemed to clog up everything from the bikes' wheels to our eyes and feet. The temperatures were soaring up again into the forties and we soon ran out of water. It was so searingly hot that it seemed somehow unsurprising that in the distance, bang in the middle of our route, we saw what looked like a huge grass fire.

As we got nearer its heat grew more intense, and we tried to turn off the track in search of water, any water, before it got dark. Our route took us right near the fire, but as we cut through the nearby jungle, the fire lit up a glimmering, shimmering mass. I began to understand how people hallucinate in the desert when they're dying of thirst. But then, dimly, we could make out the sound of snapping jaws. It could only be the sound of crocodiles, which could only mean that there really was water there. Talk about good news and bad news.

We crouched down at what was really only a stagnant pond. As we knelt down to fill our water bottles, I tried not to think about the now-familiar snapping sounds. But looking up I could see, shining through the gloom, three large pairs of eyes. The crocs were just the other side of this small expanse of water. Quickly we filled our bottles. Wondering quite what we'd just collected, I held the contents of my bottle up to my headlamp. It looked like muddy Coca-Cola. And it tasted far worse. Praying that we hadn't given ourselves an obscure waterborne disease, we lay down for an hour of much-needed sleep.

By the time the sun came up, seemingly moments later, the sky seemed to look much darker than it had done the previous day. Could it be that, incredibly, the darkness meant cloud – and therefore water? It could and it did. As the rains started we looked up to the heavens and felt our bodies were absorbing the welcome wet like sponges.

Soon after that we had to navigate a river. Still feeling the pain from the preceding days, I decided we'd use our bikes to support us as we swam upriver – the air in the tyres kept them on the surface of the water and progress was quite swift. So much so that I was able to look around.

For a moment my brain didn't compute what I was looking at. Was it a particularly thick tyre, a tractor tyre perhaps? Or the root of a tree, somehow growing into the middle of the river? Then I realised it was an anaconda. And I could see there were lumps in it; it was eating something. Something almost as big as itself. My mind flew back to a video I'd once seen of an anaconda eating a cow. I tried not to think about it, and just concentrated on swimming as smoothly and calmly as I could, even though at one point it was no more than three metres away.

As we got to the mouth of the river I was dimly aware of people fishing on the banks, and I was also dimly aware that they were gaping open-mouthed at us. Yup, I thought to myself, we are probably as mad as we look. But I also felt a great respect for the people who lived here – a country that was doing its best to chew us up and spit us out like the anaconda I'd just left behind.

Maybe that burst of adrenaline had got to me, though, because almost as soon as we got back on the bikes, I felt the exhaustion and fever come back. The sun had come up now; the heat was unbearable and the sand was making the going harder than ever. Unable to ride my bike uphill through the sand, I started to push it. I was starting to feel all the classic symptoms of severe heatstroke – the fever, faintness and exhaustion that I felt couldn't be explained by anything less. Trying to get back on the bike, I collapsed instead by the side of the road. Once this had happened three times, Jonas pulled me up and tied a towline to his bike. This helped for a little while, but I was feeling weaker than I could ever remember feeling, almost as if my body was about to shut down. Trying hard to concentrate on staying upright, every muscle straining, I began to hallucinate. This, I found myself thinking, must be how it feels before your body gives up and you die.

And as soon as I allowed myself to think of dying I felt a far greater despair. For this I'd be leaving behind the light of my life, Helena, my lovely Philippa and brand new Thor. And for this I would leave Arthur, whose life had been saved – and transformed – by our friendship.

In the heat of the jungle, and the hallucination of my fever, I could now see Arthur just ahead of me. Just as clearly as if he were really there. He was walking slowly and steadily, looking neither to the left nor to the right, just walking with a quiet determination in the way that he had when we first met, seeming to know that where he went I would follow. Tensing every muscle, I somehow found the strength to put one foot in front of the other, walking along the path that Arthur seemed to tread in the vegetation.

'OK, boy,' I said under my breath. 'If you can do it, so can I. I'm not going to give up any more than you did. You and I are not done yet.'

From somewhere I found the strength to finish that last stretch. As I crossed the finishing line, I looked up at the sky and gave Arthur and my family a silent thank you. I couldn't wait to get home and give them a thank-you hug in real life.

DOG'S NAME: *Billy*

AGE: *12*

OWNER: *Ann*

FROM: *Nowzad, Afghanistan*

LIVES: *Hertfordshire, UK*

'Billy has come a long, long way to be our dog. I have always been a dog lover, and grew up with them, and even though my husband didn't, we always wanted to get one. We knew we could never buy a dog from a shop as we'd learned all about puppy farming, but for a long time we were living in a small flat that the rescue charities we went to said weren't suitable for their dogs, so when we finally moved into a house we couldn't wait to adopt a rescue! Our first dogs were two Westies: Daisy and Tommy, who made it to the ripe old ages of fifteen and sixteen.

I'm a volunteer fundraiser for Nowzad, a charity that rescues stray and abandoned animals in Afghanistan, so we were only ever going to rescue from there, really. I'd been so moved by the stories I'd heard of the animals out there, and the way some of them were mistreated. But when we saw Billy we weren't even looking to adopt a dog – we thought we'd have a couple of dog-free years so we could enjoy a few more weekends away in Europe! It was all over when I saw Billy on the Nowzad website and loved him instantly, and before I could even mention it to my husband he came home from work and told me about a dog he had seen on the Nowzad website that he liked – who turned out to be Billy. Billy was an older dog – almost twelve – when we saw him, and after reading about his background and how he came to be in the shelter we just desperately felt we wanted to give him a good retirement home. It's very expensive to get a dog over from Afghanistan, and as Billy was older we thought that not many people would want to adopt him and he'd be left in the shelter to see out the rest of his life.

Sometimes when I look at Billy I find it incredible to think what he's been through. Billy is quite the war veteran. He bravely served in Iraq in 2006/2007 and was transferred to Afghanistan in 2009, where he worked as an explosive detection dog. He was sent to Kunduz province in 2015 and was working there when the Taliban took power. Unfortunately, when this happened Billy's handlers fled, leaving him in the hands of the Taliban. We don't know what happened to him during this time; all we know is that when the government forces retook Kunduz City and Billy was returned, he was extremely fearful of men and was unable to work any more. Billy, who probably saved many lives in his time, was given up on and left to live in his crate until Nowzad rescued him and put him up for adoption.

As anyone who's adopted a dog from overseas knows, it's a long, complicated and expensive process. Once we'd decided to adopt him, Billy finally arrived in the UK on 1 December 2016 after spending his three months' quarantine in Afghanistan. He landed at London Heathrow Terminal 5 at 7.20 a.m., and five hours later he came through from the Animal Reception Centre. When we got him home he ran around the house at 100 miles per hour sniffing absolutely every square inch of it – because he's an ex-explosion sniffer dog he's constantly checking for bombs. But now he's realised that we don't have any in our house he's calmed down a lot.

Considering his background, Billy is remarkably well-behaved. The only time he really goes crazy is when my husband leaves the house, as they've formed a really strong bond. He was extremely well-trained from his time in service, but I also think that being an older dog he is just that bit calmer, and happy to have a family. He is very food-focused (his particular favourite is naan bread) and he doesn't have much in the way of table manners, but in fairness to Billy he hasn't really needed them.

For an old dog he's incredibly energetic and gives the younger dogs at the park a run for their money. Explosion sniffer dogs are often rewarded with tennis balls, and Billy goes absolutely mad for them. It's all about the ball. But he's also incredibly loving and often just wants to snuggle up beside me on the settee.

You'd think an older dog would have outgrown their puppy silli-ness, but Billy makes us laugh on a daily basis. Only last week we took him on his first ever holiday to the Norfolk coast. We decided to let him roam the property we had rented at night so he could sleep wherever he wanted, and everything seemed fine. But when we were lying in bed on the first night we heard a loud noise and wondered what he was up to. When I went to see where he was and what he had done, I discovered that he'd jumped into the bath and was standing there with his nose pressed against the shower screen, wondering how on earth he was going to escape this situation!

Having Billy has taught us that a rescue dog really can make the perfect companion, and that there are so many wonderful dogs that deserve a loving home. And it's not just about the dog – it's great for people too. We've always said that 'a house is not a home without a dog', and with Billy here, we have a home again. All Billy wants now is to be loved from the moment he gets up in the morning until last thing at night. And he is.'

DOGS' NAMES: *Ted and Zigge*
  Stardust (aka the B Boys)
AGES: *Ted is 6 and Zigge is 2*
OWNER: *Caisa*
FROM: *Ireland. Ted is from a*
  rescue centre called Dog Rescue
  Coolronan, and Zigge is from
  Maureen Scanlon in Sligo.
  They were adopted through
  FriendsForever, a Swedish
  charity.
LIVES: *near Stockholm, Sweden*

'To look at my two boys, Ted and Zigge, now, you'd never guess what a rough background they're from. I've always had dogs, as both a child and an adult, and my dog before the B Boys was a rescue too – I've never wanted to buy a dog when there are so many unwanted dogs in the world. I live in a small town in Sweden in a flat with my son, which might not seem the ideal place for two dogs, but I live near lots of great places for dogs to run about, so I started looking into fostering.

I know it seems strange, but there are a lot of dogs from Ireland that need fostering, and there is a Swedish charity, FriendsForever, that coordinates this. The first dog I got a call about was Ted – Dog Rescue Coolronan in Ireland had got a message about a Border Collie chained up 24/7 on a farm and went there to get the owner to surrender the dog to them. When they rescued Ted, they realised that he was blind and were worried they wouldn't be able to find a home for him, so they asked me if I wanted to foster him. I'd never had – or even met – a blind dog before and I started to look for information online, but didn't find much. But I decided to go for it anyway.

Ted arrived in 2013, weak, confused and thin. He'd been kept outside his whole life and was baffled by being in a house. He'd never even walked up stairs. As a blind dog, Ted had to 'map' our home when he first arrived, walking around and memorising the layout (the first day he arrived he peed in the living room while still figuring out where everything was, but he very soon learned). Due to his upbringing he wasn't really used to human interaction, especially cuddling and touching, but we just let him adjust in his own time. Since he couldn't see us, every time he woke up I'd say, 'I'm here, Ted', because I was worried he wouldn't remember where he was. But somehow it was never a problem – Ted just handled everything I put in front of him. He's that kind of dog; incredibly cool and calm. And two days in I realised I didn't want to foster him. I wanted to adopt him.

Two years later I got a message about a similar dog living in awful conditions, rescued by Maureen Scanlon: another blind Border Collie, tied up outside a farm. He was apparently terrified and hadn't even been given proper food. I immediately said yes, and pretty soon he arrived in Sweden. We called him Zigge Stardust: Zigge because he couldn't walk straight and Stardust because he has a cataract in his right eye. Zigge was a very different dog to Ted. He was so scared, hiding in the back of the crate, and was just very overwhelmed by the whole thing. It took a long time to gain his trust. He couldn't seem to get the hang of the stairs at all, so I carried him for the first weeks, and he was so used to being outside that he couldn't calm down indoors in the beginning and just walked round and round, stressed out. To begin with I had to have him on a leash indoors to get him to calm down. But he really enjoyed belly rubs and being close to me, and gradually we started to get somewhere.

I have had to put a lot of time into training Zigge to teach him to do things like climb the stairs and deal with sounds outside and into lowering his stress levels. Obviously with a rescue dog there is more chance of them having behavioural issues if they come from a difficult background, but I do think these can be fixed with time and patience. Zigge was scared of many sounds (and I don't think it's because he is blind, just because he had no social experience when young), and I have spent days sitting beside him at scary places for him, with lots of people and cars going past. My philosophy is: Yes, I see that this scares you, but we are going to do it anyway! Until your body and mind stop thinking "flee!" and you can calm down. Zigge has come so far, but it is work in progress. It turns out that he is a very stubborn dog underneath all that stress and low self-esteem, so training takes longer!

One unexpected side effect of adopting Ted and Zigge is that they've kind of become ambassadors for blind dogs. Before I adopted them I tried to find out as much as I could about blind dogs, but there really wasn't much information out there – basically everything just said, "It can work, as long as you always keep them on a leash and walk the same paths." But that's not been my experience with Ted and Zigge – they can do so much more than that. I started posting videos on Facebook for my friends and family to see, of them playing and just living their lives, and people said I should create a proper page for them, so I did. I didn't expect such an overwhelming positive response! People would come to the page because they'd been told that their beloved dog was going blind, and wanted to see what their quality of life could be like. Eye problems in dogs are increasing in Sweden, but there aren't many people (or dogs!) showing that, actually, a dog can live a very good life without vision. Some people said that when they'd discovered their dog was going blind, lots of people – experienced dog people – had said they should be put to sleep. But Ted and Zigge show that that doesn't need to happen. The Blind Boys' Facebook page is a great community of dog lovers, and we've even met up with some of them so Ted and Zigge have new friends from all over.

Seeing my dogs now, living in a flat in Sweden, climbing stairs, walking on the leash, going in the car and being trained to use their noses, has taught me that nothing is impossible; it just sometimes takes a little longer. It's been such a joy to see their personalities develop over the years. Ted is still the cool, calm teddy bear, always following me around with a squeaky toy, which he loves (the rest of the family enjoy the constant squeaking less). When he meets other dogs he immediately knows what they're like, but even if they're scared, or tough aggressive males, Ted isn't bothered – he just walks away. Zigge's personality has revealed itself more slowly. He's still scared of loud noises, but he's pretty independent and happy these days, and loves exploring the world on his own. When he'd been here about a year, he suddenly started to get very talkative, and now whenever we're doing something he likes – going on a walk, meeting friends, eating – it's howling time! He also has a special new trick where he throws himself on the ground when he doesn't want to go home. You can pull the leash all you like, he's not moving . . .

Blind dogs see with their hearts, and there's nothing quite like the knowledge that you've made an animal happy. And they make you happy too, so if you have the time and patience, adopt a dog! They will give you so much back, and you really are saving a life.'

DOG'S NAME: *Camila*

AGE: *Roughly 5*

OWNER: *Mariela*

FROM: *Amigos de la Calle,*
  Heredia, Costa Rica

LIVES: *Florida Keys, USA*

'In Costa Rica, where I grew up, the street dog population is very high, so our family had always adopted dogs straight from the streets. I got my first street dog as a teenager and I never went back; they are survivors, really smart dogs who have learned how to read humans, can sense the good and the bad in people, and when they find the love of a family they won't let it go.

These days I live on an island in Florida Keys with my husband, but we came across Camila because she was being fostered by my mum back in Costa Rica. At first, my husband didn't feel ready for another dog as we had recently lost our German Shepherd – we don't have human children, so our pets are our children, and to lose this one was devastating for both of us. But we knew at some point we were going to adopt a dog, so why wait? So we went to Costa Rica to meet Camila personally.

Camila had had a terrible start in life. The first picture I saw of her was one my mother sent me: she was tied to a short chain in a house's back yard elsewhere in my mother's neighbourhood, with no food, water or shelter. In Costa Rica the rainy season lasts nine months, and she was clearly suffering. It was later discovered that she had a broken leg, too. After lots of phone calls it turned out that Camila was already on the radar of an animal charity, Amigos de la Calle, and had been taken to hospital to have her leg fixed, but was in that house as a transition because they couldn't find anyone to foster her. So my mother took her. She stayed with my mom for a year, letting her leg heal and getting better, but my mom hadn't really planned on having a dog – and we wanted one.

Once we met her, I knew she was right for us, although my husband wasn't sure initially. But she'd spent a year living in Costa Rica, and I was afraid of how she was going to react when we got her home. After all, she'd only met us a couple of times, she'd never seen the ocean and I have a cat in the house.

I should have been more worried about the journey from Costa Rica to Miami, however. I think she had a horrible and stressful journey that, with plane cancellations and other problems, meant that it took over seventeen hours. When the plane landed at 2 p.m. it was extremely hot and humid, and when I went to take her out of her crate she was growling and very aggressive. I quickly put a leash on her and offered water and food, but she didn't want anything.

I drove her to a nearby park where she went to the bathroom and drank a little bit of water, and when we got back to the car she rested on my legs. I could tell her stress levels were really high, but if I made any attempt to pet her she would growl at me. I was getting worried this was not going to work after all, given everything she'd been through, but I wanted to have hope. Two hours later at home we took her for a short walk at the beach and showed her her food, her water and her dog bed. She immediately went to the bed and lay down like she knew it was her place.

Initially, though she got very close to my husband, she was a very shy dog, who never played with toys and always seemed to be waiting for us to give her a command. This made me sad, as I wanted her to be like any other dog. I wasn't sure if she was unhappy or just confused. She was very shy with strangers and would charge at people who wanted to pet her, so we had to be very careful with her in public places. Now, after two years, she understands that people just want to give her love and she is the one who goes closer to strangers to be petted. She also knows how to have fun now! We got her a doggy pool, which she loves – she loves everything to do with water – and we also managed to teach her to paddleboard.

Once we were able to help her get over her fears, we could see Camila for who she really is: a playful, loving, smart and sensitive dog. We believe she is so thankful that she tries to do everything right for us. She's also very protective of us, and was so right from the start. On our first trip to Costa Rica Camila had slept at the foot of the stairs, but one night she came upstairs and woke me up. It was the first time she had ever done that, and she wasn't barking, but almost crying and placing her paw in my face. I didn't know her well at the time and I thought she was just not used to seeing me in her house, so I dismissed her, but then she went to my mom, who went downstairs thinking she might need to go outside. When she walked by the kitchen Camila stopped, and my mother realised that she had left something cooking in the kitchen that was about to catch fire.

And last year when we were on vacation in the Smoky Mountains National Park, getting ready for an early morning walk, I turned around and there was an adult black bear about eight feet away from us, looking right at us. I was frozen and mesmerised by the beauty of the animal – as a biologist I have a deep appreciation of large mammals – but I was very worried about what Camila might do. Very slowly, Camila walked over and placed herself in front of me. She never barked or growled, but I think she was ready to protect me. Slowly I pulled Camila close to me and we walked to our cabin without losing sight of the bear. Thankfully he left and went on into the woods.

The best thing about Cami is that, like many dogs, she is a constant reminder of the importance of being thankful for what we have and enjoying every moment. She seems happy all the time, and enjoys the simple things, like her pool after her morning walk or a simple ride on the paddleboard. She is such a great companion, and an irreplaceable part of our family.

To adopt a dog is the best decision you can make. It will change your life for ever – they bring so much joy and they appreciate the love and safety of a family because of their past experiences. Another advantage is that almost all stray dogs are mixes, so they don't suffer with the congenital health problems that pure breed dogs can. I think humans have a lot to answer for when it comes to dogs' suffering – whether that's inbred dogs from puppy mills, or stray dogs on the street. So if you love animals, why not to be part of the solution instead, and give a homeless dog a family?'

Chapter Two

No Going Back

'More powerful than the will to win is the courage to begin'

Ecuador, November 2014

Getting into the boats for the final leg of the race, I was reminded yet again what a compact and uncomfortable thing the kayak is. Even if it isn't pitch dark, as it was this time, it is always a challenge to assemble our kit, pack it in the boat and get ourselves balanced and ready to push off. But this time I wanted the whole process to go on for ever. The last thing I wanted to do was get into the boats and push off.

I knew that behind me, standing a little way back, the dog was watching as we made our preparations. After nearly two days with him I knew that he was exhausted and weakened by the terrible wounds on his back, and I strongly suspected that he had used up all his strength on the short swim that he'd had to make crossing the river a few hours earlier.

Slowly, still trying to eke out the time, I helped Staffan put the boats in the water. Pitch dark as it was, I knew that no one could see how I was biting my lip to stop myself blubbing out loud. This is it, I told myself, he can't follow us now. It'll be too much. He'll just go back to wherever he came from, and it will all be over. I'll never see him again.

Trying hard to focus on the job in hand, I got into the boat behind my teammate Simon. Pushing off from the bank, I made myself put my paddle in the water in synch with Simon's. Think about the race, I tried to tell myself. Think about how we must make up time on this section, how important it is that we push on, how being too slow on this section will finish our hopes of a good result for ever. Think, I told myself sternly, about how you've spent the whole year working up to this moment, and how nothing – nothing – must get in the way of making up time on this stretch.

Gripping the paddle tightly, I pushed hard against the water and our boat moved forward quickly and surely.

Two more strokes and we left the bank well behind us. But still my ears strained against the noises of the water and the crowd on the bank.

And then I heard it. A single loud splash from just at the point on the bank where the dog had been standing. I allowed myself to look back. Sure enough I could make out the dog's head as he paddled hard and determinedly towards our boat.

I turned round, knowing that we needed to push on quickly to catch up with the others. I gave another pull on the paddle and let myself look round again. The dog was now further behind, but, seeing the distance between us increase, he seemed to make a Herculean effort and speeded up.

My next stroke was not so strong. I knew in my heart of hearts that I was trying to give him a chance. Looking round again, though, I could see that the last effort had been nearly too much for him and he was falling behind again.

In that second, I realised that this was one of the most important moments of my life. If I did this thing, I told myself, I must do it properly. This was for ever. This was a moment in time that would always matter – for all my life I would stand by whatever happened in the next few minutes.

'Stop,' I said to Simon. He stopped paddling and looked round, puzzled. But I was looking behind us. In those few moments, the dog had pushed forward hard, as if he knew that this was it, this was his chance, and his life depended on what happened next.

Gradually he got closer, his head falling a little further under the water with every stroke. Then he was only inches away from the side of the boat. I leaned over. Putting my arms round the freezing, wet dog, and using all my strength I pulled him up into the boat with me.

This is it, I thought to myself. This is it for life.

Örnsköldsvik, Christmas 2015

As I jogged gently down one of my favourite hills above our house, I could see Arthur trotting in and out of the shrubs either side of the rocky path. It seemed like he was on a mission, but I rather suspected that he was just taking in the odd smell before he got to the main event – the lake at the bottom of the path.

I watched him speed up as we got closer to the water. He'd been out and about for a couple of hours, and I guessed he'd got quite hot. He ran full tilt into the edge of the lake and started to splash about in the icy water with what I could swear was a smile on his face. Now that he was soaking wet and bouncing around like a puppy, you could see how lithe and energetic he was. His love of water was now a far cry from those life-or-death struggles in the Ecuadorian river.

Sitting down on a large nearby stone, I settled down to watch him. It was incredible to think that he had lived so much of his life in a hot and humid climate. He had been part of the family for nine months now and he'd experienced most of the weather that my part of the Swedish High Coast could throw at him. And he seemed to like the cold most of all. Although he was yet to see the really deep snow that we tended to have at the very beginning of the year, he'd had plenty of freezing weather to get him used to the idea of ice and snow.

He seemed to revel in the cold December mornings, when we could all see our breath and had to dress ourselves in layers of warm clothes. On days like that, as soon as he was let off the lead he'd be off in a blaze of white on white – like the flash of a camera, everything a bright reflection of white fur and snow except for his flying orange ears.

Sometimes, in his eagerness to get outside, and especially if he thought there was the slightest danger of him being left behind (there wasn't, of course), he would hurtle out of the front door and be suddenly taken by surprise by the slipperiness of the ice. He'd be moving so fast that at least one paw at a time would skid and slide under him. It was, I would think to myself, lucky he had four legs, or he'd be falling over all the time.

But soon it was time for us to head home. Christmas was only three days away – Arthur's first, and Thor's first too – and there was a lot to do.

When we got back, Helena was in the sitting room with Philippa and Thor. They were gathered round our first ever advent calendar; two stuffed toys called Mr Moose and Mr Deer, who were both dressed with special little Christmas gifts. 'Only three more days to go – there, look at them.' Helena was guiding Philippa's hand to the last remaining presents. Chuckling with delight, Philippa opened a gold parcel.

I watched them all, mother and daughter holding each other close and talking cheerfully about their favourite present and what games they were going to play, Thor sleeping and Arthur looking on, just content to be with his family.

It *was* a happy time, but sometimes it was hard to conceal my nagging worry. Brazil had been tough, as tough as any race I can remember, and our results had reflected that with an overall finishing position of ninth in the world.

That had not been good enough for Peak Performance, and just a week before they had announced that they were withdrawing sponsorship from the team. It was a blow. Not an unexpected one, but a blow for all that. We had used their sponsorship and our own money to fund the – substantial – costs of the race, and without a sponsor for future races we were going to have to either think of some way to earn money to pay back the debts, or find new sponsors fast. As a professional athlete I don't have that many options open to me. Generally speaking, Sweden is a tough place in this respect: if you are a very able athlete you get to go to college and do your sport, and are hugely encouraged to be the best you can. But that's all you do – you don't, unlike in the US for instance, complete another degree that you can fall back on when the sports stops. And, in most sports, you tend to have to stop relatively young. That's why life can be very, very hard for some Swedish athletes after they've peaked.

So I knew that January was going to be hard for us, and it also didn't help that I was nowhere near physically recovered from the Brazil race. It always took me a while to get over a championship race, and I was still weakened by the sleeplessness and exhaustion of those seven days.

Then I looked over at Arthur, lying on his bed with his head on his paws, and thought about the book that we'd been asked to write: the story of Arthur and me. It was wonderful that people wanted to know more about him, and about how we'd found each other, and it was a fantastic distraction to be working on the book and reliving those moments in the jungle.

I looked at Arthur as he concentrated hard on licking his front right paw. In a way, I thought, he was now helping me, just as I'd helped him.

I have never loved Christmas as much as I do now. Being with Helena as we watch Philippa play, and holding Thor close as he sleeps at last after a noisy day, is as close as it can get to heaven. And of course we are only complete when we have Arthur lying in the corner, or sitting on our laps, or licking clean his smart new black Christmas bowls.

Those black bowls had been the subject of much

debate. Arthur, perhaps because he is an old soul, doesn't really do toys. So we knew we'd have to give him a serious present, and what could be more serious than the thing you eat and drink from? We'd found these beautiful black bowls, and decided to give them to him straight away; it didn't seem fair to make him wait till the actual day.

The next few days seemed to go by in a whirl of activity, not least because interest in us – or, more accurately, Arthur – seemed to be as great as ever. All the Swedish media seemed to want a shot of Arthur and me, Arthur and the children, Arthur and Helena . . . and, above all, Arthur running about in the cold fresh air of Sweden. That was fine by us, because after all it was the interest of all his fans worldwide that had got us the help I had needed to bring him to Sweden in the first place. If there hadn't been thousands of 'likes' on social media, and masses of TV and newspaper interest, who knows if the authorities would have let him make the journey.

So we were happy to have all those photocalls and to give interviews. And thankfully, it snowed. 'Thankfully' not just because it gave the photographers their best photo opportunities, but also because it has turned out that Arthur *loves* the snow. He never misses an opportunity to run about in it, and roll about in it, and then when he's had enough of that he'll stick his face full on into the middle of a pile of snow and give it a good hard rub. He'll emerge from the pile like a sort of snow monster, with all the little bits of snow sticking to his thick fur. The first time he did that Philippa fell about giggling. Not surprising really, and I'm sure Arthur knew we were laughing with him not at him.

After two days of being 'open to the public' and all the coverage it generated, it was good to get back to being just the family. And we had a very important family ceremony to perform before we headed off to stay with my mother and father for New Year.

On 20 December, we christened Thor in Själevad's church, just a few miles down the road from Örnsköldsvik. It's a lovely church in a lovely setting. In a nationwide poll a few years ago it was voted Sweden's most beautiful church, and I agree with the nation. It was a solemn occasion and for once, Arthur had to wait outside, but he behaved beautifully, almost as if he knew how important the day was.

We headed off to my parents' house in Själevad for New Year and more family gatherings – my sister and her family would be there too, so my parents would have a very full house. Unlike Helena's parents, who live in the middle of farmland with the nearest neighbours a mile or so away, my parents have neighbours quite close by. In the course of what was otherwise a very happy New Year, this became a bit of an issue with Arthur.

I guess if you're a dog you like to explore any new territory you find yourself in. When Arthur first came to live with us, he looked around the house for a few minutes, decided that this was where he had always been meant to live and immediately settled down into the bed we'd bought for him. (Helena says this is because the house smelt of me, but I'm sure he also felt it looked comfortable and manageable.) But mostly he didn't really go off on his own from that point on.

Of course, he does have a way of chasing things sometimes. Mostly cats. So he has been known to rush off suddenly and for no good reason that we can see, but he does always come back. I'm sure he doesn't understand what all the fuss is about. A dog's got to do what a dog's got to do.

But it isn't quite so easy when he's at someone else's house. At Helena's family home there's a wide area of country to explore and chase things in before he meets any neighbours. With my parents' house it is, as I say, different. There are some busy roads and also neighbours close by, and you never know what people will think about seeing strange dogs in their garden. So when Arthur went out for a bigger-than-usual explore, disappearing for longer than normal, we worried that he might have disturbed some of the neighbours.

So at the end of our stay we made a special point of going to see them to make sure they hadn't been upset. It was brilliant that they said, oh no, we loved seeing Arthur, he's such a lovely dog, we wish he'd come by more often. But still, Helena and I did think that it would be best to see if a dog trainer couldn't give us some tips for how best to ask Arthur to come back when he wandered off on one of his explores. Not *training* as such, but just getting him to come when he might be in danger.

I'm not a great reader of dog-training manuals. I suppose that with the sort of connection I feel I have with Arthur, I could 'train' him to do all sorts of things. After all, he's a hugely intelligent dog, and he does on the whole want to please me. But I don't want to issue commands to him. Although I know this makes me not the usual sort of dog owner, I think of Arthur as my equal, not someone I control. A friend of mine tells me that I talk to Arthur in the same way that I talk to my friends, and I guess that's precisely because I do think of Arthur as my friend. I know he's a clever dog, but for all that I could make him do all sorts of things like 'sit', 'roll', 'lie down' very easily, I don't want him to be someone else with me; I want him to be Arthur, not afraid or cowed like a child would be if threatened with a sort of 'wait till your father gets home' to make them behave.

Still, I do understand that not everyone in the world wants Arthur pooping in their back yards. And although I want Arthur to feel free, we did want to try to find a way of being sure that he would actually come if we wanted him to, regardless of how busy he was chasing something.

Our first session with the dog trainer was at my parents' house – we thought it would be good to have our first session in the place that had started all this off.

'It's not that we want to change anything, not that he needs *lessons*,' said Helena as she led the way into the room where Arthur was waiting for his lunch, 'but we just worry about him disappearing. Particularly where there are roads, and traffic, nearby.'

Arthur got up to greet us, obviously thinking that lunch was going to be more sociable than usual. The dog trainer went over to him to say hello. As she patted him, she said to us, 'The thing is that inside the house you have nothing that he wants, and outside the house you can't give him what he needs and that's why he doesn't listen to you. So it's a question of using voices and sounds, even the way you use his lead, to show him that you're the boss.'

She suggested that we had our own word – not 'come', because everyone is shouting that to their dogs – that he understands means that we're in charge and want him to come. The one she used with her dog was 'vieni', the Italian for come. 'Just through the tone of your voice, and how you're acting, he should know that you want him to come. He's so smart.'

We decided on 'hep'. We didn't know why, but it just seemed like the right noise.

Our trainer then set us exercises for us to practise showing Arthur who was in charge (us). The first one we tried out as soon as we got home. We both went out on a run. We chose one of those trails on the top of the hills that have all sorts of different turns and pathways, lots of occasions where you have to choose the right fork or the left. Often Arthur would shoot off down the wrong fork, and we would have to stop and find him and call him. This time we used our 'hep' formula when we got close to the fork and as we were going left or right. It seemed to work; Arthur seemed to wait for the 'hep' to see where we were going.

Excellent, we thought that evening. He's getting the hang of staying by us and waiting for our direction. We then took him on a couple of walks on the lead, not to actually use it, but so we could practise just using our voices to make him walk to heel.

After a couple of weeks, we could say 'so far so good'. I wasn't yet ready to bet that he'd come back to us mid cat-chase, but I think we'd established a few ground rules.

The big event for me in February was our pond hockey tournament. I had got together a great team of people to organise what was becoming a centrepiece of the High Coast winter sports season – two days of intensely competitive hockey between top local teams. It was a huge organisational and logistical challenge, starting with making a film of the High Coast archipelago as part of the promotion and getting posters up in every northern Swedish town with an ice rink. It was almost like a World Series adventure race in its complexity: sponsors – check; gear – check; advertising – check; team spirit – check.

I was determined that this should be the best tournament the area had ever seen, the most fun, the most competitive, the most inspiring. And I was determined that everything to do with it – food, people, lights, gear – would be perfect. It was as if I were channelling all the energy I used to use to win a race into making our tournament the champion of tournaments. The only thing I couldn't control was the weather, but ice in northern Sweden in late February was as near a thing to a dead cert as you can get.

Needless to say, I had a lot of help from Arthur. He loved running around and scoping out the ice and the snowy fields around it, although he would get impatient with the number of times I'd stop to talk to someone about some of the arrangements. I guess it's one of the banes of his life – that I will keep interrupting our walks to talk to people. Although I'd have to say that it's often his fault; when we are walking around the city we are almost invariably stopped by someone who wants to tell Arthur how beautiful he is. (Of course, I don't discourage this at all. He *is* beautiful, and I know it gives people pleasure to tell him so.)

But after all his hard work, Arthur wasn't going to come to the tournament itself. There was going to be so much noise, so much distraction and flashing lights. And, most of all, Helena and I would be rushing around all the time – making sure things were going smoothly, ironing out stuff if they were not – that I wouldn't have any time to look after him. So he stayed with Helena's parents, while Philippa and Thor stayed with a cousin of Helena's.

'It'll be fine,' said Helena, 'after all, now he understands "hep" means "hep" I won't even have to worry about him running off.'

I wasn't so sure about that, but I did know that Arthur enjoyed his stays with Helena's parents and didn't really run off that much. I thought that might be because he didn't have to go off cat-chasing, as there was already a cat in the house.

As we dropped him off the night before the tournament, I saw that there were two bowls side by side in the kitchen, one for their cat, Manda, and one for Arthur. When we came in, there was food in both bowls. Arthur didn't seem terribly interested in his. Then I saw him eyeing up Manda, who was padding purposefully over to her bowl.

As she started to eat, Arthur obviously thought he should do the same, and went over to his bowl and wolfed the lot down. Then he looked over at Manda, who'd hardly started on hers, and he must have thought, *well, she can't be that interested. I'll have hers as well.* And he went over and ate her food.

Looking on, Helena said, 'He thinks she won't eat his, so he might as well have hers.' I reckoned it was some sort of animal hierarchy coming out, where you eat the food of the animal weaker than you.

'Don't worry,' said Helena's mother, 'Manda will get her food in the end. And it doesn't seem to stop them being friends; they both sleep in the room with us, so they must all feel part of the same family somehow.'

There was no time to dwell on this rather unusual piece of animal behaviour. We left them to it and headed off into the darkness and a long night's work before the tournament started the following morning.

Come the day, and we couldn't have asked for better. We had a huge crowd of excited folk around the rinks, and some really great hockey. There were wild cheers throughout the whole two days, and I'm sure that part of that was just because everyone was having a great time.

As we picked up the children and then Arthur, we felt exhausted but happy, the sort of happy that means you go to sleep with a smile on your face.

The tournament had left me feeling relieved and pleased that it had gone so well. But only too soon it was back to real life. I was starting to try to train again, but I was still feeling weak and bad from the race in Brazil. Something was wrong, and it was making me feel low.

So one morning in March, I did what I usually do when I feel low – I took my friend Arthur off for a walk. The snow was just about the right depth for Arthur to enjoy and me to get up to a reasonable pace. I put on my headphones and set off from the house towards the trail at the top of the road that is Arthur's favourite. We marched along at a fair pace, Arthur matching my steps exactly as he always seems to do. The fresh air was doing me good, but I wasn't feeling great physically, and my mind seemed to be turning somersaults trying to figure out what was wrong.

That race in Brazil had not only taken it out of me physically, it had also done something to my head. I had so nearly been finished off by that race on so many occasions – the heat, the threatening wildlife, the sheer exhaustion, the heatstroke. And I knew that a combination of that and something else had made me less of a racer than I used to be. In my heart of hearts I knew that I had lost focus. There were so many times during that race when I'd found myself thinking of my family – Helena, the children, Arthur – and I'd made mistakes and felt weak. I wasn't as sharp as I used to be. My search for a new sponsor had been, I now realised, half-hearted. I turned round at the end of the trail and started to head home.

I had had a feeling when I left home that I needed to be alone with these thoughts. I knew this as I finally allowed myself to think what I had been frightened of thinking these last two months: it was time to stop adventure racing. As soon as I let this thought come out into the open, I found myself starting to cry. I stopped still. Arthur looked up at me, puzzled. Strange, I thought between the tears, how I seem to cry all the time ever since I found Arthur.

I set my phone to play some music. Perhaps that would distract me. It was Adele's new single, 'Hello'. I set off down the hill and headed towards the corner of our road. My thoughts were now going crazy. *It's my fortieth birthday this year, I have two small children and Arthur, who depend on me.* Could now really be the time to leave the world that had meant so much to me these past twenty years? *Is this the end?*

People had often asked me when I would stop racing, and I'd always said when it stopped being fun. And now – with the huge pressure from sponsors to win medals, and the fact that I'd been sick for months after the last race – it had stopped being fun.

Yes. It was time to move on.

Trying to imagine a world without racing brought on fresh tears. I stood at the corner of the road crying. There was no one around to see the rough, tough adventure racer looking up at the sky with tears pouring down his face, but I don't think I'd have cared if there had been.

I couldn't go back to the house like this, but the sobs seemed to go on for ages, this mourning for my past life.

Then I looked down at Arthur, who was standing silently, watching me carefully, and I thought, 'I may not have a gold medal, I may not have stood on the top of the podium, but I've got you.'

It was a thought that made the pain subside. I wiped the tears from my face and started to walk towards the house. I had made the decision. It was over. I would never race again.

Over the next few days I started to get my head round my decision (one that Helena of course supported wholeheartedly, as she does with everything I do), but it wasn't easy. And neither was it easy to talk about.

But not long after this, I found I did have to talk about it. The priest of our local church called me. She wanted me to bring Arthur and give a talk at the church about all that had happened to us. In the course of our conversation she asked me how it was all going with adventure racing.

I took a deep breath. It was time to say the words out loud to someone other than the family. 'Well, it's not really. I've retired from racing,' I said, sounding calmer than I thought I would.

'I see,' she said, although I knew she couldn't possibly 'see'. And then after a pause she asked, 'And how do you feel about that?'

Somehow, I felt that I needed to answer this question properly. She didn't understand, she couldn't, but I wanted her to. 'Well,' I said. 'Once I'd made the decision, it felt like a giant digger had come along and taken a huge scoop out of my soul. Just gouged out a big part of me and thrown it away.'

There was silence at the other end. I still felt she couldn't understand. So I said, 'You pray, don't you? To God and Jesus? You're involved with them all the time from the moment you wake up, aren't you?'

'Yes,' she said, 'yes I do, and yes I am.'

'Well, imagine,' I said, 'if someone said to you, you can never do that again. You can never pray again. Not ever again. For the rest of your life. That's the same thing for me. With racing.'

'I see,' she said slowly. 'Well, yes, I understand. I do understand.' She was sympathetic, I could hear. I think she did know then what I was going through.

When I'd finished talking to her I looked down at Arthur, who was lying on the sofa beside me. Somehow, I wanted to continue the conversation.

'But you, Arthur,' I said to him. 'I have you. We're together. At least I have you.'

He looked at me with his calm and wise expression. And it occurred to me that it was no accident that I'd been alone with Arthur when I made the decision. It was as if I could only bring myself to think about losing such a huge part of me because I was with him. And because, whatever else, I knew he'd be there for me. The thought made me feel a lot less empty and miserable.

'Come on,' I said to Arthur. 'Let's go for a walk.'

Moments later Arthur's presence had worked its magic. I was feeling a lot better.

DOG'S NAME: *Teddie*

AGE: *7*

OWNER: *Petra*

FROM: *Amigos de los Animales*
  Abandonados, Marbella, Spain

LIVES: *Åland, Finland*

'Our dog Teddie might be a rescue dog, but he has made such a difference in our lives and the lives of others that he deserves the title of 'rescuer' himself. I'd had a rescue dog growing up, and when our previous family dog died, my husband and I decided we wanted to adopt a dog from a shelter. So we started looking around on dog adoption websites and that's where we came across Teddie, who was about a year and a half old and had been rescued from the streets of Spain. We live in a village on an island in Finland with lots of forests and sea all around us, so we really wanted a dog that would love our lifestyle; relaxed but always ready to go hiking, swimming, fishing, visiting friends and family or just to enjoy the summer by the sea at my mother's cottage. A dog that could follow us anywhere and in the future be a good fit with kids. And from what the charity said it sounded like Teddie could fit the bill.

But first we had the not insignificant task of getting him from Spain to Finland. We picked him up at the airport and travelled one hour by car and two hours by boat to get home. We stopped multiple times to let him out to pee but he was so scared he didn't pee once. He lay on the back seat of the car with his head on a stuffed football the entire time, not really responding to anything we said or did. He had the same attitude on the boat, lying on the floor, not touching any of the bones, toys or treats we'd brought him. At home he found his new bed and lay down, watching us walk around in the house but not moving a centimetre himself. We were beginning to realise that Teddie's rough start had left more of a mark on him than we'd thought. We didn't know a lot about his background, but he'd been skin and bones when he'd first been picked up by the shelter and it seemed likely that at some point he'd been beaten and abused.

The early days with Teddie weren't easy. He was scared of people – men more than women – and just about everything else too. He refused to go out the door with my husband and he didn't pee for three days and didn't poop for five days even though we walked him a lot. If anyone ever raised their hand or picked up a broom he'd run as far away as he could get. He devoured his food but only when we left him alone for a few minutes. Otherwise he wouldn't touch it. We did a lot of positive reinforcement training to show him that people aren't always mean and that we didn't want to hurt him. Every time he showed a little interest in a thing or a person we rewarded him with something yummy. The task was to get him to be comfortable in different situations, no matter what happened. Funnily enough, the only thing that Teddie was relaxed about in the first few months was our two cats – he almost seemed to be wondering what kind of strange dogs they were.

Once he got over his fears, Teddie absolutely blossomed. Now he's a really happy dog who loves everyone. He struts around like he has been here his whole life and he goes crazy when he sees his favourite people coming for a visit, jumping around and whining until he gets to give them lots of kisses. He loves to sleep and often wants a pillow or a blanket to push around and make his bed before he finds the right place. It's not unusual to find him lying on his back on the sofa or in our bed with his front legs straight up in the air. He is up for anything, and wants to come with us wherever we go. One of his dog buddies showed him how to fetch a stick and now Teddie loves to chase after anything that we throw for him to fetch. He even loves to swim if it means playing with a toy.

Of course, now that he feels so comfortable with us he's comfortable being mischievous too, which does get him into scrapes. I remember one time we forgot to properly close the gate to the kitchen when we went out and Teddie wormed his way in and, for reasons known only to himself, tried to get a frying pan from the stove. We came home to find him with a cut on his forehead from where the frying pan had hit him when he'd finally managed to knock it off the stove, but he was otherwise fine, and had perfected his 'I didn't do anything' look. Another time we left Teddie at a friend's house when we were out of town for a dog show with our other dog. The dog-sitter had let him loose in a forest nearby to let him run around freely when Teddie saw a rabbit and went after it. The dog-sitter couldn't find him and Teddie was too far away to hear him calling for him. A while later I got a call from our neighbour saying that Teddie was sitting on our front porch with no leash on and looking very happy to see her. She put him in our fenced-in garden until our dog-sitter could come and get him. Well, at least we know now that he knows how to get home if he ever gets lost in the forest . . .

It isn't just our lives that Teddie has changed for the better. In 2013, I applied for Teddie to become a Friend Service Dog for the Finnish Red Cross. He (and I) got tested, evaluated and approved for service as one of the three first rescue dogs in Finland – and in the whole world, as this was a new programme for the Red Cross. Now we volunteer to visit schools, kindergartens, service homes and similar places to cheer people up. Teddie loves doing his job and being petted by people who appreciate his company. This eleven-kilo dog will jump up into the lap of an elderly person and stay there for half an hour as the old man or woman tells him their life story. I've seen old and sick people forget their pain and get the sparkle back in their eyes when Teddie puts his nose on their arm to suggest they might like to scratch his head some more.

He is such a loving dog with a big heart and he knows exactly how to make you laugh, or how to make you feel better by putting his head in your lap if you are having a bad day. I am so proud that my dog, a former abused and homeless dog, can light up the world for those who need it, and I'm proud to help him do it. Teddie also gave me the push I needed to get an education as a dog daycare manager and to start my own doggie daycare. He's given me so much, and this is my way of paying him back and helping other dogs have a better life by enriching their day when their owners are at work.

If you're thinking of adopting a dog, I'd say do your research – adopting a rescue dog is both hard work and a privilege. Make sure you pick the right dog for your family and do not give up even when your training seems hopeless. The dog will thank you for it. Teddie has taught me so much, but most importantly he's taught me that hope is never lost and that hard work pays off and can change a dog from being at one end of the spectrum to the other. And remember, when you adopt a dog you actually save two dogs – the one you are adopting and the one who gets to take its place at the shelter, so more dogs can find their families.'

DOG'S NAME: *Sparky*

AGE: *14*

OWNERS: *Lorraine and Sappho*

FROM: *Dogs Trust, Norfolk*

LIVES: *Norfolk, UK*

'I've had dogs my whole life, but actually it's my late mother Lorraine's dog, Sparky, whose story has stuck with me as a great example of the joy a rescue dog can bring. Sparky was rescued by my mother from the Dogs Trust at Snetterton in Norfolk in 2005. He was approximately one year old, a crossbreed with Border Collie in him, and the story they were told by the Dogs Trust was that he had been found abandoned by the side of the road – they think he was probably dumped. The name on his collar was Yaris (imaginatively named after a make of car). My mother, who had always had great empathy with animals, had spent some time with him in his kennel at the Dogs Trust, and they had formed a strong bond by the time she took him home. She quickly renamed him Sparky – which suited his character and temperament well.

Sparky was clearly a bright dog who had been given the rudiments of training, and he responded quickly to my mother's training sessions and very soon became an extremely well-behaved dog. He watched my mother closely and for some time didn't let her out of his sight. He was highly nervous though and didn't like men at all – in the early stages he would bark whenever my father came into the room, which caused a bit of a problem; but I think he worked out quickly that my parents were a package and he came to trust my father. Any other men outside the family circle remained deeply suspect though.

He loved toys, but mostly he adored games where human interaction was involved – a game my brother devised, which basically involved sneaking two fingers from the tip of Sparky's tail up to his nose, drove him wild with excitement – and he also loved playing with my two dogs. Anything involving chasing a ball was a delight to him, because he would invariably catch it first as he was considerably more intelligent than my two dogs and would watch the direction I was throwing it in, whereas the other two would have already started running madly round in circles looking for it. However, he wasn't great on going for long walks, even as a young dog – my parents at this stage were quite elderly so I would usually take him with him my two if I was going on a hike, but after the first ten minutes or so he would suddenly stop, fix me with a beady stare and then simply turn round and go back and wait by the car. Deeply exasperating as it was, I think he possibly didn't get enough exercise as a young dog to build up stamina. Or else he simply wanted to get back home, where his mistress was.

He had about ten years with my parents where life was fairly steady and routine. They moved around a lot but he went everywhere with them – I think they only put him in kennels a couple of times, and that was with my dogs. They adored him, and he knew it. He was talked to, fussed over, given treats – my father, who had grown up in the Australian bush and had always had a workmanlike attitude to dogs, completely changed with Sparky. When my father got ill in 2014 and spent several months in hospital I think he missed Sparky almost as much as he missed the rest of us.

At that stage we didn't fully realise it, but my mother was developing dementia. My father's illness and death in 2015 made it a lot worse, and Sparky became a lifeline for her. Although we tried to help her the nature of her illness made it very difficult to communicate with her, and Sparky seemed to be the one creature who could really get through to her. After my father died she would often sit in her chair staring out of the window, lost in some place we couldn't reach, but Sparky would go and sit beside her and rest his head on her knee and she would hold him to her. She would sing to him, and he listened. When humans were failing her due to their own grief and lack of understanding, he seemed to sense what she needed, and gave her comfort.

When she went into a care home in 2016, she couldn't take him with her. Ken, a family friend and a dog lover who Sparky knew, took him as I couldn't take another dog at the time. We did manage to take Sparky to see her in the home a couple of times, but it wasn't a success, mainly because Sparky didn't trust the staff as he didn't know them – and tried to nip one.

His instincts were all about protecting my mother, and I think he was confused as to why she was there with a lot of strange people, some of whom were not particularly welcoming to him.

My mother died a few months later, and Sparky stayed with Ken, though I still saw him a lot. Our story has a twist though – a couple of years later Ken very sadly died too, and Sparky was found by the police, who handed him over to the RSPCA. When we heard, we asked the RSPCA if we could take him – our two dogs had passed away by this point so we were able to take another dog, though to be honest even if we hadn't we'd have found a way. So he is now back with us, where he is completely at home, as he knows us well from staying with us and seeing us over the years. He is about fourteen now, we think, and still up for chasing the birds in the garden, barking at the postman and just rolling about on the grass. He often comes up to me and just rests his head on my knee; not demanding anything, just wanting to show his affection. Ken used to say that I probably reminded him of my mother. Maybe it is just that he knows I am family, and he is safe.

For me, animals can give comfort in a way no human can and they can communicate in the most basic, emotional and raw way – and I have never seen this more clearly than with Sparky. They give us their love, which is unconditional. They draw us out of ourselves, and root us in our real feelings, whether they are joy or grief. I think Sparky was extra-sensitive because he had had a traumatic early life, and he loved my parents even more because they had rescued him and given him years of stable and happy life. And now, even though we've both suffered losses, we love and comfort each other.'

DOG'S NAME: *Ada*

AGE: *2½*

OWNERS: *Alice and Ross*

FROM: *Battersea Dogs & Cats Home, London*

LIVES: *London, UK*

'I grew up with dogs and really missed having one as an adult. It can be tough having a dog in the city, but when my boyfriend and I both found ourselves working from home in London, in a flat with a garden and a sympathetic landlord, we suddenly realised we could do it. It actually never crossed my mind not to get a rescue dog – growing up my family's dogs were rescues and I hated the idea of going to a breeder and getting a pedigree dog when there are so many lovely dogs in need of a good home.

We registered with Battersea Dogs Home – we knew we wanted a small, youngish female – and as luck would have it Ada popped up in their rehoming gallery the very next day. She's a Staffordshire Bull Terrier, which is a breed that gets loads of negative press, but when I went to see Ada (with a friend because Ross was at work) she just leapt at us and immediately covered us with kisses. Ross came to see her with me the next day and she did the same thing – she was completely soppy and affectionate, as a lot of Staffies are. To be honest, once we'd both met her I don't think it ever crossed our minds that she wouldn't come home with us.

Once all the admin had been sorted we took her home on the train, which she handled like an old pro. When we got into the flat I remember us all settling down on the sofa quite naturally, and Ross and Ada both falling asleep and snoring in unison. It all seemed remarkably easy – too easy, as it turned out. When we went to bed that night we left Ada in the kitchen and she immediately started howling, and kept it up all night. The thing with rescue dogs is that something negative has to have happened for them to be in that position, and they need time to get over it. Ada had ended up without a family because her owners had split up; she'd been well-treated and trained by them but she had terrible separation anxiety to begin with. As well as the night-time howling she'd destroy cushions and pee everywhere if we left her alone, even just for five minutes. She'd get so stressed that she'd worry at her skin and had lots of sore and bald patches. We called Battersea about it and they gave us loads of advice on how to train her to deal with being apart from us, and now, a year and a half later, she's so much better at dealing with it (though she'd rather be with us 24/7).

The best thing about having a rescue dog is that you don't just change their life; they change yours. It can be lonely and intro-spective being a freelancer, but Ada needs a walk every day so we have no choice but to get out of the house. And it's impos-sible to feel alone when you have a dog around; she's intelligent and very enthusiastic about everyone and everything. There is nothing remotely aloof or understated about her. She wears her huge heart entirely on her sleeve. (Also, when I'm working Ada sleeps under my desk and is an excellent foot warmer in winter.) Caring for something is hugely rewarding, and Ross and I both feel that there's a whole new dimension of love, affection and happiness in our lives now Ada is in them.

Of course, no dog is perfect, and Ada has had her share of scrapes. She is a serious face-licker, which some people mind more than others. And she is not exactly restrained. Last summer she leapt right up onto a wooden table where people were having a serious meeting – the table was covered with architectural plans and important paperwork – and Ada barged around, licking everyone's faces and jumping about on all the paper. But she never fails to make us laugh. She absolutely hates water and I'll never forget the time when we took her to the park and she raced into an algae-covered pond thinking it was grass, and just stood in complete shock for about thirty seconds covered in algae.

If anyone I knew was thinking of getting a rescue dog, I'd say: 'Don't rule out Staffies!' And I'd also recommend going to a well-run charity like Battersea, where they do a really thorough analysis of their dogs' personality and potential behavioural problems and can offer support, as well as helping find the perfect dog for you. Now that we have Ada, I can't imagine life without her. She's so happy and good-natured, and constantly reminds us of the good in the world. Ada is absolutely bursting with love and affection for every living being she comes across and becomes completely devoted to anyone who shows her attention – and we are devoted to her.'

Chapter Three
King Arthur Conquers England

'If you want victory, then prepare for the fight'

The jungle, Ecuador, November 2014

As soon as we'd all sat down – collapsed – on the ground, the dog seemed to think it was safe to do the same. Looking round at the four of us, sitting stiff with exhaustion and hunger, his legs suddenly folded beneath him and he lay on the ground, clearly barely able to keep his head up. But once he'd decided we weren't going anywhere any time soon, he put his big head on his paws and closed his eyes.

Now that he was still, I could see only too well that the wounds on his back were deep and filled with dried blood. Every bit of fur was caked in mud or blood, and I could see that he seemed to have teeth missing from his lower jaw. But desperate though his situation was, and terrible though his condition was, he still had the most extraordinary dignity. It was as if dreadful things had happened to him, but they'd made him wise – not mad or frightened. He seemed to bear his wounds and his hunger with a kind of stoicism. Even as he lay there, half dozing, he had an aura about him.

Once we had decided that he needed food more than we did, I had this insane idea that we would present it to him on some kind of huge leaf, so that it would look like a tribute, a gift. I wanted him to know that we respected him and were going to look after him.

I took myself off into the jungle to find what I wanted. And as I searched for the largest and best leaf a jungle could provide I thought about the dog and his aura of power, wisdom and dignity. He wasn't the leader of a pack – he seemed to be the ultimate loner when he'd found us – but he still had the air of a leader. A king even. And then it came to me – like King Arthur, the legendary leader of old. I remembered a film I'd seen many years before, and being struck by the power and presence of the king.

Arthur, I thought to myself. He's Arthur.

Örnsköldsvik, Spring 2016

To fill the hole in my life left by my decision to retire from racing, I decided to throw myself heart and soul into hockey. It had been twenty years since I'd played seriously, and I wanted to recapture that magic, and perhaps share some of my experience with younger players.

The team I wanted to join was mostly made up of guys roughly half my age. They were fast and fit, if a little undisciplined. But I knew that what I might lack in speed, I could make up for with my attitude and experience – and maybe also by helping with their business and their sponsorship. But first I needed to get back in shape. I decided I would set up a training regime that would get me right back to full fitness. It was high time I did that; I'd been back from Brazil long enough.

Before I'd set out for Brazil, just the previous November, my heart rate was only 34; I knew I was super-fit. But now, after a few training sessions, I soon discovered I still hadn't recovered from Brazil. Something was definitely wrong. After some of my first training sessions my heart rate went up. And it wouldn't go down. The doctor told me that my stress responses were out of synch. Adrenaline was flowing in to respond to stress, but the off button wasn't working. Apparently, I was like a car with tyres inflated at different rates . . . Eventually the lack of balance would damage me, and without rest I'd be in trouble. I guess I was lucky that this particular thing was the only long-term bad result from a lifetime of pushing myself. Plus it was curable with the treatment programme the doctor gave me.

Once I knew what was wrong – and that it could be fixed – I decided that now was the time to scratch a very old itch. It might have been twenty years since I'd taken my hockey gear out of the locker room, but I knew I wasn't done with the game yet. I talked to the team, Husum, and they agreed to take me for a try-out. Over the next weeks, I found myself so nervous before every practice – more nervous even than when I was on the starting line of the AR World Championships.

And then one day they said they wanted to keep me. It was a great day – somehow, to make it into the team twenty years later felt like an even bigger victory – but I knew it was the beginning of some very hard work to keep the place I'd earned.

It was great to be back playing hockey – I felt happy and proud that I had the courage to go back to it after so long. I loved everything about it: the brotherhood, the late-night training at the rink, the smell of the equipment, and the sound of stick on shin pad at the start of every game. I was also proud to be able to contribute by getting some of my old sponsors to help the club by providing new jerseys.

But in between playing hockey and trying to get back to total fitness, I was actually spending a lot more time than usual sitting at my desk. By March and April we were in the final stages of getting together the book that told the story of Arthur and me.

It was a whole new process to me, and I was lucky to have the help of the talented writer Val Hudson. But mostly it was an extraordinary experience to relive the story of our struggle in such detail. I found myself sitting over the keyboard far into the night crying over so much of it, remembering our first meeting, our struggles, the terrible uncertainty of not knowing whether Arthur and I were going to make it and be together. And then, even though I knew it ended happily, more floods of tears when I relived the separation for quarantine, the worry over Arthur's operations, the rage and despair I felt when the Ecuadorian and Swedish authorities seemed to be in league against us being together.

The whole process made me wonder all over again at the magic of our chance meeting. I know there are plenty of moving stories of dogs being rescued from awful circumstances by a mixture of love and determination. But I knew that the story of Arthur and me was not just an extreme example of that; it was also unusual in its sheer unexpectedness. After all, most people who rescue a dog *intend* to rescue a dog. I, on the other hand, had absolutely no intention whatsoever of rescuing a dog when I set out for Ecuador. Having a dog, even one I didn't have to fight to bring halfway across the world, hadn't even entered my mind.

Ours was, I found myself thinking throughout the process of the writing of the book, such an extraordinary chance encounter. I had had no idea Arthur existed, but now that I'd grown so close to him I had come to wonder if perhaps he had been looking for me all along. His utter determination to follow me and the team, to be with me, whatever the cost, must have been born of some kind of knowledge that we were meant to be together. I was no expert in dog behaviour but even then, even in the middle of the jungle, I realised that Arthur's incredible determination – and the way he found strength to carry on even when he was so weak and wounded – was unique.

Eventually, the writing and the crying were finished, and we were ready. After the final proofs were passed, seemingly moments later I had a copy of the beautiful English edition in my hands.

The publishers told me that the demand to meet Arthur among his British fans was phenomenal, and that the media were queuing up to help them do that, and that we needed to go to Britain. Getting us all (we were only ever going to do this as a family) on the right planes with the right paperwork was going to be a challenge – but I guess we were used to those.

It was time to plan our trip to the UK: King Arthur was going to inspect one of his kingdoms.

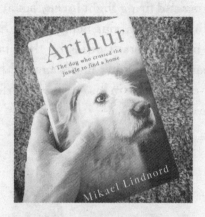

If there were any chance of my having had time to forget the trials and tribulations of plane travel with Arthur, the preparations for our British publicity tour brought them all back.

I thought we knew all there was to know about the process of vet checks, kennels and flying with a dog, but right up until the last few days before we were due to leave, we were still filling in forms, and double-checking everything with the airlines, the publishers and the Animal Reception Centre at London's Heathrow Airport. Plus Helena had to pack for Philippa and Thor too. Even though it was May, we expected London to be grey and wet, because isn't that what it's always like in London in the movies?

But eventually we were ready. And so were my parents, and my friend the photographer, Krister. Packed and eager to be off, we were quite a party, but we didn't really have much idea of what to expect when we got there.

It was a long and tiring flight for us, but at least Arthur seemed perfectly calm about being put in a kennel and taken away by strangers. I guess by this stage he knew that our separation wouldn't last long, and he was, after all, perfectly comfortable in his small but perfectly formed temporary home.

What we hadn't bargained for, though, was Stockholm Airport removing the carefully glued-on 'dog passport' that we'd stuck on the top of Arthur's kennel. So by the time we arrived at the airport, late at night and weary from a sleepless twenty-four hours, we seemed – unwittingly – to have brought an illegal immigrant into England.

These days, Arthur is just a part of the family. He comes everywhere with us, and we can't imagine life without him.

Arthur living up to his royal name on the Höga Kusten, the High Coast of Sweden.

London was a media whirlwind, with TV, newspaper interviews, events and radio. But Arthur took it all in his stride.

The Lindnords (minus Thor, who was sleeping) at Piccadilly Circus. It felt like Arthur wasn't the only one who had come a long way.

For a dog from South America, Arthur loves the cold weather and the snow. He joins in all our trekking and camping, though he wasn't that interested in digging up water.

In the run-up to Christmas, Arthur was happy to play St. Lucia for us, at least for a little while.

Arthur has been gentle with Thor from the moment he was
born, but now they have become fast friends.

Philippa and Thor both love Arthur like a brother, and
I am so glad they get to grow up with him.

Making the most
of the Swedish
summer time
with a family
picnic.

Arthur admiring his number 1 spot in a bookshop on his Swedish tour.

Arthur cool as ever before his TV appearance on STV1. He was an old pro by this stage.

Arthur kicking off the first Arthur and Friends charity run.

Relaxing in one of my favourite places with my best friend.

Our lives have changed so much since we met,
but our friendship is exactly the same.

Thank goodness I had, in my eagerness to record our adventure, taken a photo of the kennel with the passport in place. After two hours of delay and questions, it was that that saved us, and which meant that eventually, at about 1.00 a.m., we arrived in our rented apartment off London's Fitzroy Square.

Like Arthur's kennel, the flat was small and perfectly formed, I guess just like a flat would be in Stockholm. Space is at a premium in any capital city, and we were lucky to be so central. Arthur padded happily around, and after a quick inspection seemed to pronounce his new London quarters satisfactory.

We were just settling down when Arthur declared that he wanted to go out. Sometimes I do almost forget that I am responsible for making sure Arthur's had enough toilet time. I think that might be because I've always regarded him as a grown-up friend who is wonderfully self-sufficient. Not necessarily someone who I am in charge of emptying.

Although it was now nearly two in the morning, I grabbed his lead and we headed off into the silent streets. A run and a poop later and we were heading back to the flat when I realised I'd forgotten to take a key or my phone. Everything was shrouded in darkness, and I was reluctant to wake either my family or our new London neighbours in the middle of the night. For a moment, I had visions of Arthur and me spending our first night in London curled up together on a street corner, just like two strays huddled together for warmth. But sense prevailed and, after waking Helena and having a fitful sleep, the media circus began.

The first interviews were down the line on the phone and not too taxing – except for the interviewer who thought I came from Finland. (He seemed to go on for ages about how beautiful Finland was. It was really difficult to say politely that actually I lived in quite a different country on the other side of the sea.)

It was only on the second day that we properly emerged blinking into the London light. We were due to have a 'launch lunch' with everyone involved with the book and then do various interviews and a research call with the BBC. This was where they'd talk to me about the *BBC Breakfast* TV show in Manchester the following day. Without wishing to frighten me, the publishers had already told me how very important this was. I was glad that I was no longer the blushing, awkward young man that I used to be. That young man would have been incredibly nervous and could well have frozen in terror at the thought of everything riding on an interview in a major TV studio watched by hundreds of thousands of viewers.

'Come on, Arthur,' I said, holding his best red lead firmly in my hand. The flat was now littered with all our belongings; with two kids under the age of three there gets to be an awful lot of stuff. I was anxious that we didn't lose track of the red lead.

As I clipped him up ready to go the lunch, I thought that it was probably safe enough for him not to be on a lead. Unless a particularly tempting cat suddenly appeared on the pavement – unlikely on the busy Marylebone Road – Arthur wasn't going to leave our sides. But still, in the cool light of a May morning, London looked very unfamiliar. Nice, but strange. And I just didn't like the thought of Arthur being anywhere other than very close to me.

Helena got Thor into the buggy, and Philippa into her new pink outfit. Although it wasn't going to be her appearing on television, we had thought she should have special clothes for her first visit to London.

'London's so much nicer and greener than I thought it would be,' Helena said as we walked towards the restaurant. We'd taken a detour through Regent's Park, and had passed through some very grand terraces of enormous houses. I reminded myself that it wasn't just Philippa whose first visit to London this was – it was Helena's too. 'I thought it was going to be grey,' she went on, 'but it's not, and some of the buildings are so beautiful.' We'd already walked around the area a lot, and it did seem to us that London was a whole lot more spacious and good-looking than we'd expected.

Arriving at the restaurant, which was actually a restored old pub with lots of big wooden tables inside and out, we met up with my parents, with Krister, Val, and all the people from the publishers and the agency. Although it was near a very busy road, and the pavements were quite crowded, it was amazing how Arthur seemed to take it all in his stride. It was just as if we'd popped out for a walk in Örnsköldsvik; he padded along beside me, not particularly looking around, just stopping every now and then to inspect an interesting smell on a lamp-post. I suppose he thought everything must be fine if we were all together, and since he was there, well, he had better check out where the best doggy smells were to be found.

If he had been an impatient kind of dog, I guessed he would have been getting impatient by now. Because so far pretty well every human he had met had wanted to make a great deal of fuss of him – in the street, in the restaurant, in any shop we went into, or in the park. We'd been told to expect a lot more of that once he had been on the BBC, but I decided to be relaxed about that. Arthur seemed utterly unfazed by any aspect of what had been happening over those last two days.

It was nice to have a gathering to celebrate the book with so many of the people who mattered – to us, and to the book actually happening. At the end of lunch I stood up and made a speech to thank everyone for all that they'd done. It wasn't my best speech, mostly because Arthur got a little disruptive, and decided that he'd had enough of sitting at my feet and wanted to say hello to everyone else within trotting distance. His smart red lead dragging behind him, he wandered off just as I was making my best joke, to see if the people on the table behind wanted some help with their lunch.

Order had to be restored soon enough because we needed to set off to the London studios of the BBC to do some more interviews. After those were done there was just time to go into the publishers' office to meet Arthur's fans there before we caught the train to Manchester.

I'd been warned that all the companies in the office – a huge building with a roof garden overlooking the River Thames – were packed with people who couldn't wait to see Arthur. As we walked over there from the BBC and I looked down at Arthur trotting composedly by my side, I reckoned that perhaps compared to all those press conferences, and the crowds at the airport that he'd faced when he first arrived in Sweden, this was probably all in a day's work.

The publicist told me that the building's authorities said that Arthur could come into the building as long as he was properly under control in Reception. Well, that was easy. With him firmly on the lead, we went to Reception to collect all our passes. I think you're supposed to hand them back when you leave the building, but I already knew that all of ours were going to go firmly in the family scrapbook. 'Visitor: Arthur Lindnord' in its plastic lanyard was going to be part of our family history for ever more.

When we got to the top of the building there were crowds of people by the lift, waiting for a glimpse of our hero. As usual Arthur took it all in his stride, and submitted in his usual calm and gentlemanly fashion to being patted and stroked by an endless stream of smitten young publishing executives.

But then he must have felt restless, because he raced off to the other side of the floor, had a quick inspection, raced back again and then raced off again. So we decided that before the speeches began we'd better take him up to the roof garden to let off a bit of steam.

There, with views of St Paul's, the river and some huge skyscrapers in the background, he and Philippa ran about at top speed. Arthur decided that the chocolate in Philippa's hand was his by rights and bounced around barking in a 'surely you should give me that' kind of way. (In fact, Arthur knows that chocolate isn't for dogs, however hardened their digestive systems are by life in the jungle. But it doesn't stop him begging for it, or even sniffing and licking it in an experimental way.)

But we were on a schedule, so we needed to get on with the speeches. I went inside and started to get ready to talk. I wanted us to be standing in front of a shelf that had nothing but our book and Stephen King's new book on it (it was amazing to see them side by side). I looked round for Arthur. He'd been incredibly noisy a moment ago, but now there wasn't any sound or sight of him. And then I looked round a corner to a passage that led to the huge glass-walled boardroom. Now I could hear a sound. It was a long, hissing sound. Arthur, with his back leg sticking up against the glass wall of the boardroom, his face a picture of concentration, was having one of the hugest pees I've ever seen him take.

Ouch. But thank goodness for the universal love of Arthur. Laughing indulgently, lots of people grabbed paper towels and managed to get rid of at least most of the sogginess. Messages were left for the cleaners that an important bleach job would need to be done in the morning.

I suppose I should have made sure that Arthur 'went before he went', but I guess it's just yet another sign that I think of him as a grown-up friend who can look after himself. But there was no harm done, and we went into the display area for the speeches.

I'm pretty sure that, just as I had in the restaurant, I made a good speech – I remembered to thank all the right people, to make the right comments about how extraordinary it was that there we were in London celebrating a dog who'd followed me from the other side of the world; I talked about what an amazing thing life is, that a dog can go from being an abused, kicked and wounded stray in South America to being treated like royalty in London. And that was the point at which neither I nor anyone else could hear what I was saying. Arthur started barking with such ear-splitting enthusiasm that we rather gave up on the speech. And anyway, it was time to get ready for his first ever train journey.

I woke up ridiculously early the following morning, properly puzzled as to where on earth I was. The answer – a hotel room in Manchester near the BBC studios – came to me very slowly. For a moment, the strangely anonymous nature of the hotel room made me think that I must be en route to some race on the other side of the world. Then I heard a snuffling noise from the bottom of the bed. Arthur was having a wriggle. And I remembered that this was our big day on television.

Not surprisingly, Arthur had shown a polite but unruffled interest in the whole process of train travel the evening before. He had followed me and the publisher and publicist into our designated carriage, and settled himself down right in the middle of the aisle. I was about to try to get him to move out of the way a bit, but soon realised that everyone loved having him there. It just made it easier for all the other passengers to come and say hello.

He'd loved the taxi journey to the hotel in a different way, because this time he was able to sit by the window and see out. This is an unchanging characteristic of Arthur when he's travelling in a car. He doesn't seem to mind how comfortable or uncomfortable he is, as long as he can see out. It was something I realised that very first time we'd gone together in a car on the journey from the jungle to Quito, the Ecuadorian capital. Arthur settled down quickly enough, even though it must have been his first car journey – or certainly his first proper, long car journey – and was quite happy as long as his head was high enough out to see out. Not head-out-of-the-window like you see some dogs doing in cars on the motorway, but just so that he could see what's going on.

'Hey, Arthur,' I said to him. 'Time to get up. It's our big day today. Lots of people are going to see you, and we've both got to be on our best behaviour.'

His tail thumped against the side of the bed, almost as if he knew it was a big day and he was looking forward to it. He was looking very smart with his new fur-cut – I'd decided he looked way too furry for a spring trip to London, and he'd had a proper trim. He still looked beautiful and golden and fluffy, but not quite so wild and furry as he had a week or so before. I gave him a bit of a hug, and marvelled yet again at how incredibly luxurious his fur was and how he seemed to shine with health.

We arrived at the studio half an hour later. I could tell that the editor and publicist were really tense, even though they did their best to pretend that they took Swedish athletes and rescue dogs to television studios all the time. The publicist said it was the first and probably only time she had emergency Bonios in her bag ready for when her author wanted one. I took a moment to wonder how people did this kind of job. It must be so stressful shepherding people around and hoping the trains weren't late, that people didn't say something outrageous, or failed to turn up, or were rude to the interviewer . . .

Twenty minutes later, I could see them getting a great deal more tense. We were doing an interview with a BBC children's news programme before the main event of *BBC Breakfast*. They were smart new studios that all the people showing us around were obviously very proud of. For some reason Arthur was at his most bouncy, bitey, nosy and mischievous. He started by running off and checking out a big state-of-the-art camera at the corner of the new set. As he nearly knocked it over giving it a few exploratory bites, I could see the BBC studio managers starting to look a bit nervous.

I suggested that he'd be better once we were sitting together on the interview sofa with the interviewer. He wasn't. The first thing he did was to start play-fighting with me, putting his mouth round my wrist in the way that he has. Then he started jumping on and off the interview sofa, and then he decided that the interviewer, a young man who was doing his best to pretend he found all this absolutely charming, needed to play as well. By the time Arthur had his mouth softly round the whole of the interviewer's arm, I decided enough was enough and lifted him (Arthur) on to the floor.

In the end, it was actually a great interview (and the out-takes were very popular on Twitter!), but we were all mightily relieved that it was pre-recorded, so some of the liveliest bits could be edited out.

But it couldn't be edited out for the main event. The *Breakfast* show went out live, so if anything disastrous happened the whole nation – or the bit of it that would be watching TV at 8.50 a.m. – would see it. We had half an hour to go before our slot, and Arthur was still bouncy. So I did what I so often do when I can feel something difficult getting more difficult: I rang Helena.

'Why don't you do what the trainer said, and take him out and bond with him for a bit, and maybe he'll let off steam and calm down?' she said. I thought that sounded like a really good idea, because at the moment it seemed like Arthur wanted my undivided attention. So I put him on his lead and took him on to the pavement outside the studios.

What the passers-by going into the building to start their working day thought I have no idea. But within moments Arthur and I were jumping about, with me turning this way and that – 'Arthur, come!', 'Arthur, here!' – with Arthur jumping up at my raised arm, barking away and having a wonderful time. Ten minutes or so later it felt like we had both let off steam, and I led him back into the studios.

As we waited in the wings for our slot, there was a sports correspondent finishing off his international report with a piece about golf. Arthur, only feet away although out of shot, started whining a little. The cameras swivelled round to film him waiting to go on.

'Uh-oh,' I thought, 'he's still got things to say. This could go either way.' But I had my emergency dog chew with me, so as we went on to the sofa Arthur was distracted to begin with.

In the end, the interviewers were lovely, the show felt really good and to top it all Arthur behaved beautifully.

We got back on the train to London feeling pleased and relieved, and then pleased all over again when we were told that sales and enquiries for the book had rocketed since the broadcast. There was one more big piece of media to go the following morning, but for now we could have a bit of a rest when we got back to London.

Except there was never really a chance to rest. As soon as I was back at the apartment, Philippa and Thor were all over me – 'Daddy's back, we can play now' – which was lovely, of course, but it meant there was never really a moment to stop and recharge.

I realised that for all that we adventure racers are trained to go without sleep, there are different sorts of sleeplessness, different sorts of ways to get tired. And being on show and talking in English was tiring in its own unique way for me. Arthur, on the other hand, seemed completely and totally himself. Not a trace of difference in his behaviour here in England; it was just as if he could be absolutely at home anywhere in the world as long as we were together.

That was the thought that I took with me when I eventually went to sleep that night. And when I woke up, still tired, I was still thinking that thought, so I felt ready and able to manage the big radio interview that morning.

When we arrived at the studios, everyone was really welcoming and good to us, and didn't mind that we goofed around a bit in the studio, taking some shots of Arthur about to do his first Radio 4 broadcast.

I think the show went well. It wasn't that easy to be part of a two-hour conversation about all sorts of things that meant very little to me, but I think I did justice to our story. At any rate, Arthur seemed very happy, and settled down by my feet for the duration, unperturbed by all the voices and general activity.

After that, we had a day of enjoying London as a family. Exhausting though the tour had been, it was great that everything had gone well, so we set off on the Sunday determined to make the most of our English trip.

We decided that there were very few things more English than the Changing of the Guard. It meant we would get to see Buckingham Palace when it was the centre of a ceremony. The only other piece of live English history I was familiar with were the aggressive debates I'd sometimes seen broadcast from Parliament. It had left me with a slightly sceptical attitude to English traditions. And I know I'm not alone in Sweden in finding those scenes in the House of Commons a bit like a zoo or a bear pit.

But as we made our way through the thick teeming crowds towards the Mall and Buckingham Palace, we were bowled over by the splendour of the buildings and then, when the band struck up and the Regimental Slow March began, we were bowled over by the grandeur and elegance of that too. I think Britain should have a bureau to put out images and pictures of things like this; stop showing Parliamentary debates – just have the Changing of the Guard on a loop!

I was also amazed by how easily my family adapted to this unfamiliar place and the huge crowd. Throughout the walk, and as we wandered about through the crowds to find the best place to observe the ceremony, the children were excited but not at all alarmed by anything. And Arthur walked between the legs of these hundreds and hundreds of people as if he'd walked on English pavements in huge crowds ever since he was a puppy. And when people stopped us to say, 'That's Arthur, isn't it? He's the stray you rescued ... oh, isn't he beautiful?' Arthur took all that in his stride too.

Afterwards we headed back up to Regent's Park where we thought Arthur could have a bit of a runabout. We'd said we'd be there on our Instagram in reply to lots of Arthur's fans who knew we were in town, as we thought it would be nice to give people a chance to say hello to Arthur in person.

As we approached the part of the park where we'd said we would meet people, a man in his fifties came barrelling towards us. He looked extremely emotional, and for a crazy moment my brain went into defence mode. But he wasn't going to attack me; he just came straight up to me and shook my hand.

He seemed to be trying very hard not to break down in tears. Hardly able to get the words out, he said, 'I had to come. I had to come and shake your hand. I've read your book.'

I started to say something – like thank you, and I hoped he'd enjoyed it. But he carried on: 'I read it in one sitting. It's changed my life.'

He looked hard at me, and then down at Arthur. Still trying hard not to cry, he said, 'I had to get on a train to meet you. From Glasgow. I've been travelling all day. But I had to meet you. Shake your hand.'

He was so overcome with emotion now that I didn't think anything I said would have sunk in. But as I started to say how touched I was that he'd been so affected, he just turned round and quickly walked away to the edge of the park and disappeared into the distance.

'That was extraordinary,' said Helena. 'He came all this way, and then he could hardly say what he came to say. But it is amazing, isn't it? The effect your story has.'

We both looked down at the cause of it all. Arthur was for once sitting still, and looking up at us expectantly. At that moment he was more interested in having another run round the park than listening to people talk about him. But he didn't have much time to run about, because moments later two more people – a mother and son – came towards us. They were wreathed in smiles and started talking as soon as they were within earshot.

'We are from Ecuador!' they said. 'And this is Arthur! He is so famous, we love Arthur!' And they bent down to make a huge fuss of him.

Once again, I had to take a deep breath and pinch myself. Here were two strangers from the other side of the world, joining us in the middle of London to celebrate one formerly beaten and battered dog. A dog who'd defied all the odds to find his new home.

I took a moment to wonder again at the powerful effect our relationship had had, not just on me and Arthur, but on people all over the world.

DOG'S NAME: *Lubomir Visdogsky*
(named after a Slovakian ice
hockey player), but we just call
him Lubo

AGE: *8*

OWNERS: *Erin and Roger*

FROM: *Adopted from the Mae*
Bachur animal shelter in
Whitehorse, Yukon, Canada.

LIVES: *Yukon, Canada*

'Life without Lubo is unimaginable now, but it's not so long ago that having a dog seemed like a pipe dream. Roger and I got married a few years ago and were living in big cities (Vancouver and Ottawa) in Canada, but everything changed when Roger got a job in Yukon, and we packed up and headed up to a town of 25,000 people, a 30+ hour drive north of Vancouver.

When we first moved up, we were house-sitting before finding a place of our own. That house came with a dog named Arlo, a passive pizza-stealer who stole our hearts. We fell in love with him and when we left we hoped against all reason that somehow we'd be able to keep him, but obviously we had to give him back. It really made us realise, though, that a dog was what we were missing. There was never a question of getting a non-rescue dog.

99

There are lots of dogs out there that need homes. And we needed a dog.

We knew we didn't want a puppy, so we went to the local shelter to look for an adult dog. There were a few available dogs, but we liked how Lubo was a smaller dog without being a 'small dog', if you know what I mean. We started walking him every second day. His name then was Mr Bear and he seemed sweet, if also a little quirky, personality-wise. He also didn't seem to understand how to walk on a leash, which made our trips out a bit interesting. He was listed as being between six and nine years old, but actually now we know him better we think he was on the younger side of that. He'd been brought into the shelter after being picked up by animal control. They believed he had been wandering the streets for some time, and it was December in the near-Arctic. It wasn't the first time he'd been picked up; his former owners had come to get him before, but now they no longer wanted him. There was also a history of abuse, abandonment and neglect. Despite this rough start, though, there was just something about him, something that made us feel that he was right for us. So we decided to adopt him.

As soon as we received word that our references had been checked we went to the shelter as early in the day as we could. Lubo recognised me but he loved those women at the shelter too, and when we got him home he was pretty scared. We kept him on a leash in the house because he seemed to be overwhelmed by the size of the place. We planned to keep him out of the bedroom at night but he howled all night and eventually that leash was around the foot of the bed frame and he slept on the floor beside us in the bed he had had at the shelter. There were accidents and when we got a baby gate to keep him in one part of the house, he busted through it. His submissive and anxious tendencies were maxed out when we first got him home, too, and in particular he was very submissive with Roger and had very bad separation anxiety. He'd never had any training but we quickly realised that he was smart. Maybe too smart . . .

We've worked a lot on his separation anxiety by monitoring him (he has an auto-answer Skype account) and trying numerous tactics to help with it. He's not 100 per cent but far better than before. We've had to work on his submissiveness with Roger. He's obviously very scared of the dominant male but luckily we've developed safe spaces where they can cuddle and be close. One safe space is what we call 'pillow corner' – which is pretty self-explanatory. It was meant to be a space for reading and knitting but it's now Lubo's. He sleeps there every night and from time to time we fall asleep there too. With Roger gone to work out of town lots of the time, Lubo and I spend many hours there together.

Now Lubo is doing brilliantly. He still struggles with separation anxiety when left alone but is down to just a short spell of howling and pacing, compared with nearly all day when we first got him. And now that he's more settled his personality has come out much more. Remember when we said he is smart? He was top of the class in senior dog training. It has also served him well in finding things to eat in the house. In my Christmas card this year, we wrote a list of some of the things he had eaten:

A loaf of bread, a bushel of grapes*, a half pack of hot cross buns, a facial mask, a tub of lip ointment, flour, rice, lentils, barley, half an onion**, coffee beans, half of Roger's carved jack-o'-lantern, baking supplies (graham squares, white chocolate), a jar of peanut butter (which he tracked around the house), an apple, a banana (including the peel but not the stem), about thirty guava candies (all removed from individual packaging), two chocolate bars, at least four granola bars, countless Kleenexes (many used, not all), and candles.
*resulted in a stay in vet hospital
**we had to make him puke that up as onions are poisonous to dogs

To get these things, he has broken through baby gates, baby locks, learned how to open cabinets, how to open the dishwasher and then use it to get onto the countertop . . . we caught him on camera using a serving spoon as a tool to pull down things further back on the counter. Like I said, maybe too smart.

Actually, food is a constant obsession for Lubo. We joke that he loves carbs because he's eaten more than one loaf of bread and got into the flour once. But recently, he seems to have developed a taste for avocados. A bag of them was left too close to the edge of the counter and he brought them down. We got home to find smeared avocado all over the floor, the skins and pits cast aside. He'd eaten one and a half avocados (luckily, fairly small ones). We found a third avocado half eaten in his kennel. About two hours later, he ran by with another avocado. He had stashed it somewhere! He's taught us to be tidier, because if there's food visible, Lubo will steal it.

His uniqueness is part of what makes us love him, even if the results are sometimes less than ideal. One thing we've had to learn is that we can't leave Lubo with anything that might be vaguely rope-like – as he used to be tied up outside for days in the Yukon winter before he came to us, Lubo learned to chew through the rope that held him there. This habit has turned into chewing through anything he thinks might be some sort of rope. We don't have a single reuseable shopping bag with an intact handle, we have to hide backpacks, his leashes are kept out of reach, strappy shoes have to go in the closed closet and we learned the hard way that he can't stay in the car by himself as he took out three seatbelts in a short time, ahead of us needing to drive back to Yukon from Alaska.

Because of his background he also never learned to play normal dog games like fetch (we're working on that one). Instead he likes to play a game we call 'hut hut hut' after the motion in American football where they hike a ball through their own legs. Lubo finds apple-sized rocks and does this for ages. We've bought him footballs to try to make him stop with the rocks, but he has a definite preference for the latter. He's a really great dog for an outdoorsy lifestyle though. He just loves hiking and being with his pack, and he's pretty tough – though also small enough to be carried if need be. And if we let him off the lead we know he's not going to go far because he wants to be with us.

He's such a joy to be around, and makes us laugh all the time. He gets so excited when we get home that he doesn't jump up on us but rather does spin jumps in the air. He does the same for food. In fact, we have to put his food into doggie brain teasers because his former street dog tendencies mean he will eat it all in no time otherwise. He's sweet in the evenings, just wanting cuddles, and feisty in the mornings. If our alarm doesn't wake us in the morning, he will. But he doesn't have to pee, he just wants someone to hang out with him in pillow corner.

We have a tiny teardrop trailer. It barely fits the two of us – it's just a bed on wheels. It's seven feet long so there is room at the end for Lubo. To get him down there to sleep, we throw treats at our feet and when he gets down there, we block him from coming onto the bed with our feet. It's night, so he doesn't have much fight. But in the morning he slowly, sneakily, commando crawls his way back up. You look at him and he's at your knees. Close your eyes for a moment and he's at your waist. Close them again and you've got a little spoon in your arms.

Roger had dogs growing up and I didn't, but I'm now a fully-paid-up obsessed dog person. It's the first topic of conversation and Lubo is always on our minds. To be honest he is quite spoilt now, with several walks a day and all the fanciest toys and treats. But he deserves it. We gave him a home, but he has given us so much, and taught us so much. Most importantly, he's taught us patience. He has had a rough go of life and he brought those experiences into our house. But though it has been a slow process, he continues to get better and better. You can teach an old dog new tricks, after all.'

DOG'S NAME: *Mr Digby*

AGE: *9*

OWNERS: *Allison and Scott*

FROM: *Best Friends Fur Ever*
Rescue Inc., Sydney, Australia

LIVES: *Queensland, Australia*

'My husband and I have always had dogs, and when we met our dog Digby we already had two: Mia and Roxi. Though we'd had rescue or unwanted dogs before, I wasn't particularly involved with the community, but after we adopted Roxi my sister got involved with dog rescues and got me hooked on the kind of rescue stories you'd see posted on Facebook – both the happy ones and the sad ones. My husband and I started to follow a few rescue groups on Facebook and watched their trials and tribulations, and we decided that if we could do more to help, we should.

In February 2014 we noticed that a rescue called Best Friends Fur Ever Rescue Inc. had pulled some dogs from the kill list in a pound near us. We immediately went about finding out how to help these gorgeous souls. We were not quite ready to foster, but were told we could be their sponsors, which meant a monthly payment to help fund their care until they were adopted. In March I decided to visit the Gympie shelter, which was about a two-hour drive from our place – I took a carload of blankets and food and got to spend a day bathing, walking and cuddling dogs. Not long after that, the Gympie shelter started to have issues with the local council as their noise restrictions were being exceeded. When I visited again a few months later, the council problems had escalated and now there were also problems with the landlord. It seemed likely the shelter would have to close. I was worried about the fate of the dogs when I got home that day, so I spoke to my husband and we agreed that we would foster one of their dogs and see how it went.

We all made the drive to Gympie to meet our new foster dog – his name was Digby. We had never met him before and he had only recently been saved from being kill-listed in Hawkesbury Pound in Sydney. Digby had been picked up as a stray wandering the streets of Sydney; he was microchipped but his owner never came for him. His chip name was 'Boss' and he was seven years old.

The day we met him it was raining, and the two-hour drive to the shelter had been miserable, but there was a sense of excitement in our car – Mia and Roxi sensed that we were going somewhere and it was going to be fun. When we arrived, Digby was brought out to meet our girls. He looked a bit scared – his ears were back and his tail was between his legs – but he was very submissive and our girls decided that he was allowed to come home with us.

The drive home was uneventful and Digby slept curled up in a corner most of the way. When we arrived home, he checked out the whole house and back yard, went to the toilet, then came back inside. We bathed him twice under a hot shower to get the smell of the pound off him, then he got straight up on our bed with the girls and fell asleep. He looked so relaxed and content, it was honestly like he had always been here and this was where he belonged. He wasn't unscathed from his experiences, though. We took him to the vet the week he arrived and it turned out that he had developed a urinary infection while in the pound and also a respiratory infection, which were fortunately both easily treated with antibiotics. He also had a skin irritation on his belly, which continues on and off to this day.

We got to know Digby very quickly and it became evident that someone had truly loved this boy in his previous life. He loved everything, including our girls, his food and his humans, and he had no hesitation in sleeping on our bed. He was toilet trained and had beautiful manners, and it made me wonder how he had managed to end up in a pound, with no options, but that was a story we'll never be able to uncover. By the end of July 2014 Digby had won all our hearts and we realised we had to adopt him, as we couldn't imagine life without him.

We have been so lucky with Digby; he came with only a few small issues. One is that he doesn't chew his food and sometimes chokes on it. Secondly, he wants all the attention, which some-times doesn't sit well with our girls – he will literally barge them out of the way to be the closest to us. He also cries a lot when we take him for a drive to the vet or anywhere without the girls, and he panics and whimpers. It's the same when we take him for walks, even when the girls are there; we can only assume that he might think he's going to be dumped again. He's very particular about things too, and sometimes when we don't put something away and leave it where it doesn't belong he will lift his leg and pee on it! Lastly, if we pat Digby while he's sleeping he'll growl at us, but as soon as we stop he starts whining for more.

Digby is such a happy dog it's awful to think of the possibility that he might have wasted his life in a shelter – or worse. He's turning ten this year, but he is still extremely fit, healthy and agile and we expect him to be a part of our family for a long time yet. When you see him racing around you'd think he was a much younger dog. His favourite game is the ball – he will chase it, but his preference is to chase his sisters around the yard with the ball in his mouth. Amazingly, he still manages to bark even with a mouthful of ball. He also loves water, whether it's a hose, a pool, the shower or, most importantly, the beach, which is his favourite place apart from our bed.

Digby has taught us that we all deserve second chances and I would recommend anyone considering adopting a rescue dog to get out there and do it now. We cannot imagine our life without him and hate to think what would have happened to him if a rescue had not stepped up and saved him. This boy was meant to come to our family. He fitted in perfectly right from the beginning and he will have a home with us for ever.'

DOG'S NAME: *Duke*

AGE: *10*

OWNER: *Ruth*

FROM: *Duke was found as a stray in Ireland and brought to a local dog rescue charity by the RSPCA.*

LIVES: *Bedford, UK*

'I was brought up with dogs and have had dogs all my adult life. All except my first dog have been rescues, and now I would never have any other kind. I have no children, and when I began living with the man who is now my (long-suffering) husband, he knew that it was highly likely that he might come home from work any day to find that I had added to our pack. Fortunately, we live in a large house near a beautiful Victorian park, and our dogs have always had the run of the house. I have never chosen any of my rescue dogs; two have come through my vet (who is also a good friend and knows that I'm a complete pushover when it comes to dogs needing a home), one came through another friend and one was brought to me by my parents. Duke came to me through my vet, who knew that I was hoping to rescue an Irish wolfhound. She rang me and asked, 'Would a Great Dane cross do?' When I got him, Duke was so thin that I could see every bone in his body. He had been badly beaten and was fearful of everyone, but his fear was displayed as aggression.

When I brought him home, a week before Christmas, I was totally unprepared, but the kennels where he was being kept were overflowing and I had to bring him home on the day I saw him or risk losing him. I already had two dogs at home, neither of whom were impressed with the new arrival. Within hours my collie, Billy, and Duke had got into a scrap and blood was shed. The first months with Duke were far from easy. It took weeks for him to put on any weight. He would steal any food he could reach (and he could reach pretty much anything in the kitchen!), even food that was cooking on the hob, and walking him was a nightmare. He was terrified by the noise of wheels on pavements – shopping trolleys, post and newspaper delivery trolleys and bicycles would send him into a frenzy of barking and lunging on his lead to get to them and try to destroy them. At first I walked him on his own (my mistake), but eventually I realised that by 'pack-walking' him with my other dogs he would learn from them. He did. Not only did he learn to enjoy going for walks, but the three of them bonded and there were no more fights.

I also took him to a local dog training centre to teach him how to interact and relax with other dogs. The trainer there suggested I enrol him in agility classes as he might find them more entertaining than obedience classes. She was right. He loved it. Within weeks he became the class clown. Great Dane-cross dogs are not really the right size for agility, but what he lacked in technique he made up for in enthusiasm. His weave between poles was more like a series of three-point turns, and instead of running through the tunnel, he usually got stuck in the middle and then took off wearing it. That summer, the centre held a fun dog show at which Duke covered himself in glory, even winning reserve best in show.

Duke had always had problems with his eyesight from his time on the streets, but we never realised how bad things were until he went completely blind when he was just three years old. Looking back, his poor vision probably contributed to his fear and aggression. We know that he had been very badly treated before we got him and that, coupled with his bad eyesight, must have made the world a very scary place for him. But by the time he went blind, he had been transformed by routine, discipline and unconditional love. He knew that he could trust us with his life and he did. He coped brilliantly and we just had to remember not to move the furniture around.

He has a huge and very lovable personality. People always stop me when I'm walking him and want to fuss him and know what breed he is (as a harlequin Great Dane/pointer cross he has very unusual markings). Sadly, as is the case with many large dogs, as Duke gets older his joints have begun to fail him. Last year, he had hydrotherapy to see if it would help (he pooped in the hydro tank on our first visit, but after that he quite enjoyed it). After a couple of bad falls he was no longer able to cope with hydro, and by Christmas last year things were not looking good at all. Duke was unable to support his weight on his back legs, and therefore unable to go for walks or to the toilet independently. It seemed inevitable that I was going to have to make the hardest decision of all and let him go. I've done it three times before, with previous dogs, and it never gets any easier. The heartbreak is excruciating.

But if he couldn't go for walks, or even get around the house, his quality of life would be gone . . .

But in my heart of hearts I knew he wasn't ready to chuck in the towel just yet. His back legs might have given up, but he hadn't, and if he was willing to fight then so was I. I found a company on the internet who specialise in making aids for dogs with disabilities. Duke now has his own trolley (who'd have thought that his arch-enemy would become his best friend!), which supports his back legs and enables him to use his front legs to propel himself along. He is now able to go for walks in the park and play with his rubber ball. Once again, he has coped bravely and brilliantly with whatever life throws at him, and now he has his smile back.

Duke has taught me so much. He has been the most difficult dog I have ever rescued and the only one who has shown any signs of aggression. But he has also been the most rewarding. He is an adorable, gentle giant whose love of life (and food) knows no bounds. His unconditional love and trust, considering his appalling start, are nothing short of miraculous, and I treasure every day I have with him. He's not perfect, though. His snoring is absolutely thunderous!

I will never understand why anyone feels the need to buy a dog. Animal shelters are heaving with wonderful dogs (who find themselves there through no fault of their own) just waiting for a forever home. If you're considering getting a dog, please, please, please think about rescuing one. They may not all have pedigrees, but dogs are not accessories. They are loving lifelong companions and friends.'

Chapter Four

Home Runs

'The only time success comes before work is in the dictionary'

Swedish High Coast, July 2016

Another year, and another SwimRun – the competition where pairs of athletes run the rocky trails of the islands and swim the bits in between. Sitting in our kitchen, making plans for the year's trails and routes, I was half excited, half stiff with tension worrying whether everything would go as well as I wanted it to (I always want everything to be as good as it can be, if not better). 2015's race had been a great success, even though it had ended up being slightly more exciting than I had expected – a huge freak summer storm had taken everyone by surprise, and made every aspect of organisation more complicated, and more dangerous.

But even without freak storms there was plenty to worry about. Not least keeping the many boats in the water around the islands out of the way of the racers. When the competitors are swimming between islands there is a trail of orange buoys behind them, and of course everyone around about is warned about the race well in advance. Still, there are always plenty of people out there who are new to the area, or don't know about the race, or – and this happens only too often – are drunk in charge of a boat.

One thing I wasn't worried about, though, was Arthur. There hadn't been any more occasions when I seriously worried about his running off or getting lost, and I allowed myself to think that he now knew his new home – the High Coast – as well as he'd ever known the jungles of Ecuador, and he loved being out in it.

Almost as if she'd heard my thoughts, Helena – tidying up the children's breakfast at the other side of the kitchen – said, 'I think Arthur needs a run, and so do I.' Before I could say anything, I heard a clatter and patter of claws and paws as Arthur came rushing down our wood staircase from upstairs.

Trotting up to Helena, he stood there looking up at her, wagging his tail with ferocious efficiency.

Incredible.

'That's amazing,' said Helena, looking down at him and laughing. 'He heard me. He must have understood what I was saying by the tone of my voice or something.'

'It must be like they say,' I said. 'That dogs understand what you mean just by the way you say things.'

As Helena walked out of the kitchen to fetch Arthur's lead and change her shoes, I watched Arthur follow her as if he was glued to her. Clearly, he wasn't going to miss the chance of going for a run if he could possibly help it.

A few moments later I looked out of the window and watched the two of them set off together. Arthur was going at exactly Helena's pace, trotting neatly by her side as if he were measuring her steps. I knew that sometimes dog trainers can take months to get dogs to walk to heel, but Arthur seemed to do it totally automatically. He'd walk slowly next to Philippa's buggy, or march out on a walk in the city but never pulling on the lead (unless there was an exceptionally attractive smell he had to inspect), or, if we were in open country, he would run about beside us. No, I thought to myself, I don't think he's going to leave Helena's side.

115

Örnsköldsvik, August 2016

The SwimRun race lived up to all my expectations, and it was great to have so many people telling us how good the course was, and what fun they'd had tackling it.

But in my new post-adventure racing life, I could never rest on my laurels, and I didn't want to either. Within twenty-four hours I was on to my next project, and the next sport – hockey. On summer wheels, of course, as opposed to winter skates. Perhaps I was a little long in the tooth to be playing serious hockey again – I was going to be forty in September after all – but, as the saying goes: 'You don't stop playing games when you get old, you get old because you stop playing games'. But it was great to be playing with my new and young team – Husum – and great to be involved in helping with getting kit and sponsorship. Playing games was work for me; I felt, and still feel, that every sport has the potential to turn into a project. And so, too, it seemed, has a certain dog.

We'd been approached by ESPN to make a major film documentary, and we also had the German publishers organising a film crew from RTL to come to see us at home and at play. And then after that we were due to set off for Stockholm and Gothenburg to help the Swedish publishers promote their edition of Arthur's and my book. It was going to be a very busy time, so before it all began we decided to take a few days to have our first ever family camping holiday.

The Skuleskogen National Park is one of the most beautiful parts of Sweden – it's got rocks, snow, mountains, lakes, forests and stunning views all year round. You can ski in winter, hike, swim and camp in summer. From the red granite Slåttdalsberget mountain, there are great views down over the High Coast and the Gulf of Bothnia. And if I sound like a travel brochure advertisement, that's because I've grown up with this place being on my doorstep, and I love it.

After a non-stop, exhausting few months, I wanted nothing more than to relax with my family in the middle of this beautiful place. And by the time we had the car loaded with what felt like the entire contents of the house, I was even more ready for a rest.

Last to get in the car was Arthur. He was sniffing round the wheels as if to inspect their roadworthiness before we set off, but he seemed excited, as if he knew that we were going off on an adventure. I watched him as he moved round to the fourth wheel of his inspection. Any minute now he should be jumping into the back of the car. Up until then, he had always expected me to lift him up into the car. It wasn't that he couldn't jump up himself – he always did if I wasn't around – but if I was, he'd just wait and wait until I eventually gave in and lifted him up into the car. Amazingly manipulative really . . .

But this time I was determined that we would just wait him out. Even if we were late setting off, I had decided I wouldn't lift him up, he must jump up by himself.

The back door of the car was open. Everyone was sitting in the car – Thor half asleep, Philippa playing with her pink bracelet, Helena settling herself in the passenger seat. 'Right,' I thought. 'As long as it takes, Arthur. We're on holiday, we've got all day.' Whatever else happened, I would *not* lift him up.

Arthur came round to the back of the car to where I was standing. He looked up at me. I thought I could detect an iron will there. 'Hup, Arthur,' I said, knowing full well that Arthur had never in his life jumped 'hup' into the car when I told him to.

Then, almost before I had finished speaking, Arthur quickly and calmly jumped into the back of the car, and was lying down in his favourite comfortable position before I could say another word. He put his head on his paws, all settled in for the journey, as if this was how he always behaved.

I got into the driving seat. I may have won the Battle of Jumping-In, but why was it I felt I'd been outsmarted?

We found our ideal camping place quite quickly. Just off the High Coast trail, it was on the shores of the lake, and not far from the mountain that we were all going to climb (although maybe some of us might need to be carried). There were some other tents not far away, but we liked our spot and we'd found just the right amount of shade to protect Thor and Philippa from the sun.

We set off up towards the mountain, Thor on my back, Philippa striding out in her favourite pink shoes. Arthur seemed to be sticking with us all the way, just trotting along behind and not seeming to feel the need to explore very much.

'I think he likes having us all together, don't you?' said Helena. And I think she was right. Although Arthur never seemed to be a 'pack' animal when it came to other dogs, I don't think there's much doubt that he thinks of us as his team, or pack, now.

The climb started off in the spruce forest, and then got quite rocky and steep. We made slow progress; when we got to the top, we had covered all of 3.1 kilometres – about a hundredth of an adventure racing hike! – but I loved every minute.

As we walked slowly around the rocks at the top, admiring the familiar views, I thought how glad I was that I'd made that difficult decision to retire from racing. Yes, the future held lots of doubts and worries, but we would get through all that so long as we were together. Arthur bounded around us, barking his head off, as if he could hear my thoughts and was telling me how much he agreed.

The sun was just starting to cool a little as we made our way down the mountain. We could see the light shimmering off the lake, and even the trees seemed to glint in the light. It was beautiful.

Back at the campsite we got everything ready for the night, made the tent safe and got out the food and drinks we'd bought. I thought any minute now everyone would calm down and get sleepy. But there was none of that. Philippa had to go in and out of the tent, seeing if she could see her own shadow, Thor had to explore every last centimetre of ground, just to see if there might be something to play with or anything to eat (I guessed all this was good for his immune system, anyway). Both of them kept Helena very busy.

And throughout all this Arthur padded around, sniffing this bit of rock or that, and checking that Thor's buggy wasn't going to fall into the water (at least I think that's what he was doing). I reckoned that obviously wherever we were was home for Arthur, so our new camping base was our new home, so Arthur had to make sure it was all right for us.

Eventually it grew dark, and finally everyone got sleepy and climbed into the tent. We could hear some gentle splashes as herons and cranes dived in and out of the water, and the distant murmur of voices as other families around us got ready to go to sleep.

I'm used to sleeping pretty well anywhere and everywhere. After all, sleep is a very precious commodity for an adventure racer, and you can't afford to miss a minute of an opportunity to get some. But it was very hard to sleep that night. Not because we were particularly uncomfortable, but rather because we had a guard dog who was on high alert for marauders throughout the night. Who knew whether there might be a brown bear or a lynx prowling around? But what it did mean was that whenever anyone – even over on the other side of the lake – left their tent to have a pee or whatever, Arthur started barking as if to say, 'Don't come near my family, I've got my eye on you.'

I thought it was sweet and lovely to know he was looking after us. I'm not sure the other campers felt the same.

When we got home, it was nearly time for the TV crews to start filming. But before that happened there was something I'd promised myself I would do. I already had my princess – Helena's – name tattooed on my arm, and now that we were a family of five I had to have Philippa, Thor and Arthur on me too.

I know some people don't like tattoos, but for me there is something wonderfully final and committed about the names of the people I love being literally a part of me. It was going to be a long process – eighteen is a lot of letters – but a little bit of pain was almost an essential part of my commitment. I chose a flowery lettering for my flowery little princess, big bold letters for my son and elegant regal capitals for Arthur. I'm delighted with the result, and love the fact that they'll be with me till my dying day.

Then it was time for the TV crews to come over and see Arthur living with his new family. First, the German TV station RTL sent over a film crew to show Arthur indoors and out of doors. The film would be the first big step in the book's promotion in Germany. I was getting quite used to being interviewed on camera by now; in fact we all were, and of course Arthur, who must surely have been a Hollywood star in a former life, seemed to accept it as a perfectly normal way to spend the day.

Having said that, there were definitely times when being filmed on the High Coast trail must have been very boring for him. Why would everyone stand around talking to each other when they could be running down the mountainside, or having a swim in the water at the bottom? I took a photograph one day that should probably be captioned 'Portrait of a Bored Dog'.

The German film wasn't going to be shown until the German edition was published – in early October, soon after Swedish publication – but our next visiting film-makers weren't going to show their work until spring of the following year. In August, ESPN producer Kristen Lappas brought with her the guys from Seventh TV and the journalist Tom Rinaldi. This was going to be a big production; filming would take a whole week, and as soon as they arrived it felt like there were a lot of people – and a lot of expensive equipment – all round the house.

To start with I was worried that Arthur's patience might finally be a bit tried, because these guys were going to make a proper documentary, not just about Arthur's story but also about the sport of adventure racing. But in fact it was good news for Arthur: they just wanted lots of footage of him walking and running with me, of Arthur with the family indoors and out of doors, of Arthur dashing about outside generally. In short, they just wanted to film Arthur being happy and doing all his favourite things.

I, on the other hand, was about to be a lot less happy.

The interviewer, Tom Rinaldi, is at the top of his game. He's an award-winning reporter on golf and tennis, and has written a book about a 9/11 hero. It also quickly became clear that he knew his stuff when it came to the sport of adventure racing.

When we first started talking I thought he was impressive – even though, like so many Americans and Brits, he couldn't *begin* to be able to pronounce Örnsköldsvik – and as we talked more over the course of filming, I found him to be even more impressive.

Eventually the day came for the 'big' interview. We had filmed Arthur and the family, and I'd already seen some amazing footage. They had also – incredibly – found some video footage of Arthur in the transition area in Ecuador, before I even met him.

It was extraordinary to watch. There was this young-looking – so young it did make me doubt again that he really was three or four when we met – but very, very battered dog wandering around among all the athletes looking at them one by one. Almost as if he were looking for a particular person, I found myself thinking, not just looking for food.

It was only a few seconds of footage, but I watched it again and again. Arthur looked so beaten and yet so proud. It was impossible not to feel a stinging in my eyes as I saw how he begged with such dignity, and then thought about how unbelievably well and happy he is now.

I had just been looking at that footage when Tom and the crew started to set up the scene for my interview. They checked the light, the cameras and all the usual paraphernalia, and I settled in behind the table in the sitting room to begin.

We started off well enough as I talked about how my early ambition to be a professional hockey player had never happened, and how I had come into adventure racing. I talked about how tough it was to be tough, and how in one race my heel had fallen off, and in another I had unexpectedly somersaulted down a cliff.

And then we talked about setting up for Ecuador, and soon we were talking about the transition area and the moment I saw Arthur.

It was at that point that I felt more stinging in my eyes. Of course, I had been through those moments many times, not least in writing the book and in talking to people about it all. But for some reason – and maybe it was having seen Arthur in the film footage – I was finding it incredibly difficult to hold it all together.

I kept thinking about what would have happened to Arthur if we hadn't met. Now, over eighteen months later, I knew there was no way he would still have been alive. Not a starving dog with those terrible festering wounds. And the more we talked the more overwhelmed I felt.

There were long pauses now between Tom's questions and my answers. It wasn't that I didn't know what to say; it was just so hard to actually say it. After a long pause, Tom eventually said, 'I see in your face there's a lot of emotion there.'

And it was as if a tap had been turned on. Tears poured and poured out of my eyes. I held my hand over my mouth to try to stop myself sobbing out loud. Eventually I got out the words, 'It is the single best thing I have ever done in my life.' And then just let the tears and sobs come as they would.

After that, I somehow got out the answers to Tom's next questions. Somehow. But the whole interview took well over an hour longer than it should have done, just because I spent so much time unable to speak. As I say, Tom is a very good interviewer.

We said goodbye to the ESPN folk, half sorry to see them go, half relieved that such an intense week was over. But the arrival of finished copies of the Swedish edition of our book soon made me focus on the upcoming tour to promote it. That second week in September we were due in Stockholm to do lots of television and radio, and then we were due to go on to the world-famous Gothenburg

Book Fair, where the publishers had lined up an intense couple of days. They didn't yet know that it actually coincided with my fortieth birthday, and I decided I'd keep it that way; Helena and I could celebrate that some other time.

She'd decided that she would stay at home with the children and then just come out to Stockholm for the weekend. Not just because it would have been too much disruption for them to go on a trip, but also because she had another full-time job: admin. The amount of paperwork that the SwimRun, hockey and everything else seemed to generate had to be seen to be believed. Every morning there seemed to be a new huge pile of documents and invoices. I was so glad that Helena was so good at dealing with it.

'It's just you and me, then, Arthur,' I said to him as I gave his coat a thorough pre-book-tour comb. He looked up at me in that wise way that he has when I'm having a conversation with him. I was sure that he understood we were going off somewhere together. And he put up with my fussing over his fur with his usual patience. I fussed a little bit more than usual, giving him an extra-careful brush.

As I concentrated on his golden ears, I thought I could feel a tick bite on him, which seemed to match another one on the top of his left leg. I couldn't see anything that needed attention, but asked Helena to come and take a look.

'Hmm, it does just feel like a tick bite to me,' she said. 'But we can always check it out if you're worried.'

They did feel like tick bites, but I couldn't stop myself imagining that perhaps they were something else. Arthur seemed absolutely as right as rain, but I guess the fact that I was still such a new dog owner meant that I didn't always know what was OK and what wasn't with my friend.

So the following morning I took Arthur to the vet. Apparently, it's quite common for dogs to have unexplained lumps and bumps all over them, especially when they are no longer puppies (and for all that I had thought Arthur looked so young in the film footage from Ecuador, I knew he was quite a grown-up dog).

'I think,' said the vet, 'that it's really hard to know what these lumps are. I doubt they are anything serious, but it would probably be best to take them off and have a look at them at some point. Nothing urgent. Try not to worry. But I can make an appointment for when you're back in a week or two.'

We made an appointment. I didn't really like the idea of Arthur having an operation; I could never forget how helpless and battered he had looked when he had all those operations in Ecuador, and didn't want him to go through that again if we could help it. But I comforted myself with the thought that these days he was so much stronger that it wouldn't be too much of an ordeal for him.

Still trying to distract myself from the fear I felt for Arthur and what those bumps might mean for him, I focused on packing. Smart clothes for me, favourite foods for Arthur. I liked the idea of a road trip with my friend, and it always feels great to meet Arthur's biggest friends and fans.

Stockholm, Gothenburg, here we come, I thought.

DOG'S NAME: *Golan*

AGE: *7*

OWNERS: *Patricia and Hagai*

FROM: *Beijing, China*

LIVES: *Ecuador*

'I always wanted a dog as a child, but my parents didn't. When I was very young I had a stuffed toy dog, and I remember being heartbroken when I realised that was the closest to getting a dog I was probably going to get. But as an adult I think I'd kind of put having a dog out of my mind, at least until I met Golan.

I have always cared about the environment and became a vegetarian when I was twenty-four, and in 2007, when I moved to Beijing in China, I became quite involved with the vegan and vegetarian community there because it wasn't the easiest place to be vegetarian. That's where I met Chris Barden, a Yale graduate who ran a group called the Vegan Social Club, as well as a charity called The Little Adoption Shop. Chris had been rescuing cats and dogs from meat trade trucks and the streets, and whenever he or someone in his network picked up a new pup, he would share their details with everyone in the Vegan Club and pretty much everyone else he could to try to find them homes. There is a serious stray dog problem in China, and they also have one of the highest rates of rabies in the world, so if a stray dog is actually spotted, it might be by the municipality division in charge of the city's hygiene, which means the dog will be removed and taken to a pound temporarily (future uncertain), or, worst-case scenario, it will end up in a cramped truck with hundreds of others on the way to a market to be sold alive, as dog meat, skinned in front of other terrified dogs for the consumers to make sure the meat is fresh. So there is a real need for help in rescuing dogs.

One day in July 2010, I was sent a short home video, shot from the floor up, of this tiny skinny puppy running around in somebody's living room. All you could see in the video was the floor, his legs and face. He was awfully cute, and something in me just clicked. The time was right; my boyfriend and I were financially stable, I had time to learn about and care for the puppy and a rented apartment with a landlord who didn't mind pets. The building was inside a residential closed area, with a big park in the middle where dogs of many different sizes played daily. I showed the video to my boyfriend and we went to meet the dog that same week. Mei Banfa (as he was called – it means 'no choice' in Mandarin) had been picked up from a *hutong*, one of Beijing's old neighbourhoods, starving and wet in the middle of the cold spring rain. His teeth were only just beginning to grow and he weighed about 4 pounds. We renamed him Golan there and then.

We knew we wanted him, but we were going to South Africa the next month, so we asked his foster family if they could take care of him until we came back, and they agreed. Once we got back, I wrote to the foster mum to arrange a time to pick Golan up, but she didn't reply. At all. Eventually I found out that they had decided to keep him. I can't explain how that felt, but there was a lot of sorrow. How can you be so sad to lose somebody you never had?

But two weeks later they called us to say that due to new very busy work schedules, they were no longer able to dedicate time to Golan and felt terrible about leaving him alone for fifteen hours a day. 'Do you still want him?' they asked. The answer was a resounding 'yes'.

When the fosterers dropped him off they brought dry food and a leash. We lived on the sixteenth floor, but Golan wouldn't go into the elevator; for some reason he was terrified of it and tried to stretch his four legs in all directions as far as he could and pull back to avoid going inside it. I really hoped this wouldn't be a permanent fear as that was a lot of stairs! The fosterers told us a few of his quirks, like the fact that he thought the toilet was a water bowl, would steal eggs and liked apples – but only red ones, and only if they were peeled. When they left Golan followed them to the door. He sniffed, scratched, tried to look under the door and walked around looking for a way out. He cried for two hours and nothing I did distracted him. By 7 p.m. he was not crying any more but he was sad, lying next to the door, waiting. He hadn't eaten anything all day, not even peeled red apples. I didn't want to leave him alone but by now I was hungry too so I called my favourite takeout place, Annie's, an Italian franchise in mainland China with all the comfort Italian food you will ever want. They already knew my order, melanzane with ricotta with a salad. I looked at Golan's sad face and figured: maybe some Italian will help. I ordered him chicken escalope with egg and veggies served on spaghetti, easy on the condiments, please. His dish was twice the price of mine. He ate the whole thing. And then, finally, he slept. I picked him up, and put him next to me.

Once he settled in, he was like any other puppy. Full of energy, always ready to play, never tired. We took him out three times a day: a morning walk, an afternoon two-hour playtime at 4 p.m. and a night walk. Golan is a mix of a lot of dogs, but there is some terrier in him, which makes fetching one of his favourite games. Every time I arrived home, he would bring a toy in his mouth and shake his hips (Shakira-style, as my dad says), wagging his tail.

He has such a unique personality, and so many quirks that just make him *him*. For example, he has never liked rain, and would prefer to stay indoors until the rain stops, even if this means no toilet break for him. He has actually spent twenty-eight hours without peeing because it was raining and he refused to go out. He also doesn't like men smoking – he starts barking at them as soon as he picks up the scent. But for some reason he is totally fine with women smoking! Golan is very perceptive; he knows when you need quiet time, or if you are upset. He is also pretty good at remembering everyone he meets and will enthusiastically say hello to anyone he has already met by wagging his tail and frantically shaking his butt (his hips don't lie). He follows mealtimes strictly and will never eat more than what he needs, so he has never put on weight, even when I wanted to fatten him up a bit! Golan loves speed and running around with my other dogs on the beach is probably one of his main activities during summer.

He's a very good dog for the most part, but he has got into some scrapes in his time. One of the most memorable was when we lived in a closed residential complex in Beijing with huge green areas, artificial lakes, bamboo forest, the works. At that time, we had already adopted our second dog, Lola, and had rescued two other puppies, Blackie and Brownie. All four of them loved the green areas, of course, and I made sure they got to enjoy them every day. Each building had semi-private elevators that opened directly into the private lobby of our apartment with a magnetic card. One day while I was at work, I got a call from my boyfriend saying he couldn't find the dogs – all four of them – anywhere. They'd been in the apartment with him, and then suddenly they weren't. He had looked round the emergency exits – nothing. And then he heard them, but he wasn't sure where the barks were coming from. Desperate barks, I might add. The administration was called, because we needed to go to each floor, to each private lobby, to check where they were because our magnetic card only allowed us to go into our apartment and nobody else's. It turned out there was a glitch in the elevator system, the doors got opened and all four of them had gone into the elevator, towards the green areas I suppose. Golan, Lola, Blackie and Brownie were eventually found safe on the lobby of apartment 2 on the sixth floor. Looking totally innocent, they jumped back into the elevator and happily went home.

It isn't over the top to say that Golan has changed my life. It's almost as if having him has made me open up emotionally, and made me more sociable and approachable – he's also the reason I went on to get more dogs, and I have four now. Golan has also raised the bar on what I would expect my friends to be like and I now choose more wisely who I trust. The unconditional nature of a dog's love is beyond anything you could imagine and it does both: you start giving more, but you also start expecting more. I am a much more responsible person now, too. My life has a structure. I have a fixed schedule that keeps my days running, which wouldn't happen in the absence of my dogs: Wake up at 6 a.m. Monday through Sunday, walk them (great cardio!), feed them. Be home by 7 p.m. to walk them and feed them, long walks (two hours) on the weekends, visits to the parks, keep a 'just in case' budget, plan things ahead but manage at the same time to be spontaneous with four dogs, disconnect! You can't really be on the phone all the time you are at the park with your dogs. I never carry any electronic devices during our walks; this keeps me focused on them – and the people around me, who I would have never even looked at otherwise.

Knowing that someone depends on you is such a powerful thing. Recently I went through a devastating emotional experience and if it weren't for the fact that the dogs are used to their schedule and I know they can't take themselves out and fill their own bowls, it would have been so much more difficult for me to come out from that situation. I just HAD to get up every morning and do it all over again, which distracted me, kept me grounded, kept me going and gave me a 'there is more in your life' way of thinking that really helped.

So if you want a dog, I'd say definitely get a rescue dog – but do it responsibly. It is a life you are putting in your hands, a life that needs nurturing and care, just as with any other living creature. It will be up to you what they become and that takes commitment and work. They depend on you and will literally trust you with their lives, but in return, they'll make your life so much better.'

DOG'S NAME: *Teddy*

AGE: *Between 8 and 12*

OWNER: *Joy*

FROM: *The Bresta shelter in Romania*

LIVES: *Chester, UK*

'I have always had dogs, but Teddy is very special, as he came into my life at a very difficult time. When our previous dog died in 2013, my husband Phil and I decided that autumn to adopt another dog. But before we could, Phil was diagnosed with terminal cancer, and died in February the following year. I still felt that I wanted – no, needed – a dog, and I started going round the rescue centres in my area. I just didn't find a dog I felt that instant connection with. So I started looking at different sites online, and I registered with K-9 Angels and put in my wishes: small to medium sized and mature. I was sent a few options, and when I saw the picture of Teddy – who was then called Merlin – that was it! I just felt I had to have him.

Teddy had been a street dog in Romania and a wonderful girl called Sarah from Birmingham had brought him over and fostered him until his permanent home could be found. Sarah had also brought over two other dogs, Sultan and Zeus, who were living with Teddy in the same run in the shelter. I live about 100 miles from where Teddy was, so when it was time to pick him up I asked a very good friend, Sharon, to come with me as I was worried he wouldn't travel well – I had completely forgotten that he would have travelled from Romania by road and sea! When I went to collect Teddy his shelter-mate Sultan was with him and Sharon fell in love with him – we went back two weeks later to collect Sultan too! It was wonderful because when we got Sultan back he and Teddy were so happy to see each other, and they remain best friends.

Teddy was quite agitated as we drove him home, so Sharon got into the back of my car with him to calm him down. She was successful and said he was just like a teddy bear – and that was when I decided to change his name from Merlin to Teddy. As soon as we got home I hand-fed him some dog food to reassure him, then took him for a walk. He was very interested in his new environment but nervous of people or dogs who approached us. I don't know what his life had been like in Romania, but he was quiet and reserved with me. He didn't like other people or dogs. I think that maybe he didn't know what to expect, or whether he could trust me to look after him properly. He didn't like being out when it started to rain and he'd hide under bushes until I could coax him out and get him home. There is also occasional hunting on the marshes near where we live, and a military firing range nearby, both of which made him hide in the bushes as well.

Aside from his nervousness, though, I think I was very lucky with Teddy. He seems to be a wise boy and completely understands body language, both human and dog. Initially he was very wary of people and other dogs, but I kept him close to me and talked to him, and sometimes distracted him with treats, so he learned to associate meeting new people and new dogs with a good thing. I think that helping him to get over his fears has allowed his true nature to come through, which is kind, caring and a little bit mischievous. He will still try to find a way out of the garden, even though he has three walks a day, and he's always looking for adventure. When he wants to go on an adventure I just follow him until he is ready to come back; I then put him on his lead and bring him home. I do make a fuss of him but I don't give him a food reward as I don't want to reinforce his wandering behaviour.

Teddy is such a patient and gentle dog (unless you're a cat or a squirrel). And he always makes me laugh. I remember last summer we met a Staffie with his owner and her baby in a pushchair. Teddy was intrigued by the baby's bare feet and started sniffing them. The Staffie walked between Teddy and the pushchair and gently moved Teddy out of the way. So Teddy took a few steps back and waited until the Staffie was behind the pushchair again. Teddy then went to sniff the baby's feet again. Again the Staffie came between Teddy and the baby and gently shouldered Teddy away. Teddy then took a few steps away and didn't try to sniff the baby's feet again. He knew that the Staffie was telling him to leave the baby alone. Both the owner and I were absolutely thrilled at how this situation worked out.

Another time we were in a large field and there were about five or six small dogs there, including three puppies. They were about six months old and miniature dachshunds, so you can imagine how tiny they were. Another dog in the field came over – a massive one-year-old Leonberger puppy. Teddy wasn't happy with this, so he walked between the Leonberger and all of the small dogs and kept him away from them. He also doesn't like squeaky toys – I honestly think the squeak makes him think that they're alive! He treats them like vulnerable creatures and is very gentle when he is given one. If Teddy is with another dog who has a squeaky toy he gently pushes it out of their mouth and takes it away to safety.

To me having a dog is a partnership, and even more so with dogs who've never had homes before. As Teddy was successful when living on the streets I know he doesn't have to live with me. But I believe that he is happy with me as he does usually come back when I call him. He's a true friend, and I am so happy to have him in my life.

If you're thinking of getting a rescue dog, my advice would be to make a list of all the potential problems that could be encountered. Then from that list decide what behaviours or problems are not ones you feel able to deal with. That will help a shelter find the best dog for you. And never ever be cruel to your dog. They don't have to be there – it's a relationship built on trust, and it works both ways.'

DOG'S NAME: *Gaspard*

AGE: *Approximately 8*

OWNER: *Lydia*

FROM: *Sans Collier, Provence, France*

LIVES: *Germany*

'Gaspard is my first dog, and my best friend. I work in an office, which means I spend my whole day sitting down, and I wanted to be a bit more active and get a bit healthier. I am, however, absolutely not a jogger, so when my daughter told me that shelters are always looking for people to take dogs out for a walk I got in touch with my nearest shelter and started to go for walks with a dog – with Gaspard! He was new in the shelter, and I was new to dog-walking, and we just found each other! Two months later, I had adopted him and taken him home.

Gaspard was about two or three when I met him, and no one knew how he'd ended up without a home. He came from a rural part of the South of France, where, while some people have beloved pets, there are also quite a lot of dogs that aren't really cared about and that just wander around, going wherever they like. The police have an order to bring stray dogs to the shelter and after two weeks – if nobody asks for them – they will be euthanised. Thankfully, in recent years animal lovers have set up other charities to rescue dogs from these shelters – and that's how Gaspard ended up in the shelter where I met him. Even though Gaspard had been neglected, it seems like he hadn't had too bad an experience of humans, unlike some rescue dogs, as he has always been very friendly to people and to most other dogs.

One of the good things about Gaspard and me having walked together before I adopted him was that he already knew me and was relaxed with me when I brought him home. I was very nervous though! Actually I have to be honest and say that Gaspard is always relaxed – bordering on lazy. I think because he was so laid-back he had very few behavioural issues. The only ones I can really think of are that in the first months he liked to 'protect' me, and when he was on the leash he would start to bark. Off the leash – no problem! In a group with other dogs he'll always try to be the 'boss', and in the later evening when it's dark outside, or on a rainy day, he doesn't like to go outside (though he still needs a walk). Basically he's relaxed as long as we're doing something he likes!

Gaspard has changed my life so much, and opened me up to the joy a dog can bring. Three years after adopting him, I adopted another dog, a ten-year-old called Trixie. Sadly Trixie died last year, but we had a great time together, and I'm glad I got to give her a good life in her last years. But I am so grateful to still have Gaspard, waiting for me every day when I come home from work for us to go for a walk together. We are outside every day, whether it's rainy or sunny, storm or snow. I can't imagine my life without him – he is my perfect match.'

Chapter Five

Fortitude at Forty

'Some defeats are more triumphant than victories'

Ecuador, November 2014

Stiff, flea-bitten, half blind with tiredness, Arthur and I and the rest of the team crossed the finish line of the Ecuadorian Adventure Racing Championships hardly aware that we had done so.

All those months of preparation, and stress and

tension over equipment, fitness and navigation, had ended in the most unexpected of results. Even as we trudged down that last track to the finish line, we knew that we were very far from being in the top five, or even the top ten.

Yet the real result, the one that I hadn't quite come to terms with in my head, was the fact that we set out a team of four and came back a team of five. As the four of us humans hugged each other with a mixture of exhaustion and relief, I looked down at the exhausted dog at my side. His wounds looked as terrible as ever but, weak as he was, he stayed by me as if there were an invisible lead between us.

Still in a blur, we checked in with the race organisers, and then found ourselves going straight to a tent where there were some journalists and reporters standing around four chairs that were all set up with microphones. Aiming for the nearest chair, I looked around for Arthur. Sure enough, he was just behind me. And as soon as I sat down he collapsed on the floor by my side, as if he knew it was safe to do so.

The barrage of questions began. First about the conditions of the race (arduous, tough, hard, torturous), but soon they were all asking about 'the dog' as they had seen the story unfolding on social media.

'He's called Arthur,' I said, determined that my friend should always be called by his proper name. 'And he's in a bad way. We need to get him to a vet.'

'You taking him home?' someone shouted.

My heart skipped a beat. They made it sound so simple. But I knew that there would be nothing simple about transporting a sick dog to the other side of the world – with just three days to organise it.

'I don't know,' I said.

But I did know. Arthur was coming home with me.

Stockholm, September 2016

It's impossible not to dwell on the past, even in the midst of the pleasures of the present. As we landed at Stockholm Airport, memories of that first arrival, the interviews, the battles with the authorities came flooding back. But it was wonderful to be revisiting Stockholm, with Arthur now such a firm part of the family, and it did feel like a conquering hero coming home. There were some journalists waiting for us, but the big guns of the TV and radio studios were scheduled for the following days. So we were taken to our smart metropolitan hotel to rest up ready for the next day.

Arthur and I had a room together. It made me smile to see the luxury king-sized double with crisp cotton sheets and subtle lighting. All ready for an endurance athlete used to a snatched couple of hours' sleep on a concrete floor in a transition area and his friend – who was more used to piles of rotting rubbish or the floor of a jungle.

It all felt just as surreal the following morning. We emerged, blinking, into the cold bright light of an autumn day to see all that we hadn't been able to make out when we'd arrived the previous night. The hotel had a spectacular view out over the water – and a red-carpet entranceway that would not have looked out of place in Los Angeles. Standing on the red carpet and looking out over Arthur's back to the view, I had another moment of wonder that he and I could have come this far.

And that feeling didn't stop when we set off for the TV4 studios for the morning show. On the same bill were Peter Jöback, the famous singer who got his first big break with the Abba guys, Ernst Kirchsteiger, the TV decorator/philosopher who everyone in Sweden loves – and the Red Hot Chili Peppers!

Unfortunately, as is so often the way with magazine TV shows, you all do your segments of the show

separately, so although it would have been quite a gathering on the sofa if we'd all been together, in the end my only companion was Arthur. But I think that was probably enough for everyone. Not least because it turned out that Arthur was in a particularly frisky mood.

As I was explaining a little of what I felt about our first meeting to Ebba von Sydow, our glamorous and charming interviewer, I was aware that Arthur was getting a little restless. I snuck him a meat treat so that he'd have something to get his teeth into while we were talking. It didn't last long. As soon as he'd finished it Arthur got up and gave the floor round our feet a good sniff.

I was just getting into some of the more complicated aspects of how Ecuadorian law doesn't protect stray dogs, and how cruel a life they sometimes have to lead, when Arthur made a beeline for Ebba's glass of water. With true precision and characteristic thoughtfulness he started lapping up the water in the glass, all the time being careful not to knock it over.

I carried on explaining how we hoped to make our Arthur Foundation into a source of money and support for those who are trying to help rescue dogs all over the world, but it was impossible to ignore the slurping sounds coming from Arthur as he tried to get at the water in the bottom of the glass. In the end Ebba just gave in and helped Arthur finish her glass of water.

It all ended very happily, but it made for another thing on my list of things to worry about before we did an interview: make sure Arthur's had enough to drink.

Marie from the publisher, Bonnier, then moved us on swiftly and professionally to the first of many signings. It was extraordinary to see all those copies of our book piled high. The book wasn't going to be released till the Saturday of that week, but that didn't stop the publishers getting me to sign hundreds ready to ship to those shops that I wouldn't be able to visit. We even had a special stamp of Arthur's paw print ready for those who wanted their books signed by us both.

Then from that first signing we went on to more radio interviews and more print – including some with our old friends *Aftonbladet* and *Expressen*, who had been the two leaders of the media that had helped us so much in Ecuador.

Our last big TV interview in Stockholm was on the SVT *Good Morning* show. This time I made sure Arthur had had plenty to drink – but not so much that he might be caught short when we were on air (quite a difficult calculation) – and we let Arthur have a proper inspection of the studios before the show began so he wouldn't want to prowl around during the interview.

I thought I had all the bases covered – enough water, a familiarisation with his surroundings and a meat treat just before they started filming. I think it worked . . . Arthur was very lively and wanted to play with the two presenters all the time, but then I suppose he wouldn't be Arthur if he didn't sometimes want to say hello to people.

Stockholm had been wonderful. It was great to meet so many of Arthur's fans. And after all the TV shows, everyone seemed to know he was in town and it was completely impossible to walk down any street without being stopped by someone who wanted to say hello to him. Some people asked me the question I get asked in Ö'vik – how does it feel to have a dog who is more famous than you? I say it feels great, and I quite understand that my 'fame' as an adventure racer and athlete doesn't compare to Arthur's as the nation's – if not the world's – favourite Ecuadorian emigrant.

Soon it was time to get on another plane and set off for the Gothenburg Book Fair. I'd been sent the agenda and running orders for all the events. I had always known that the book fair was a big deal, but when I saw my name in black and white next to so many distinguished writers and stars, I started to feel pretty awed. But it didn't stop me wanting my events to be the best attended and the most popular, so I was pleased to see that I was on at noon, a good slot. I guess you can take the man out of the competition, but not the competition out of the man – I would always find something to feel competitive about.

There was also a lot to look forward to at Gothenburg. Not just the excitement of seeing so many famous faces, but also the knowledge that there would be lots of Arthur's fans who were making special efforts to come to see him. It was also a great place to be – not just for the fair itself, but also the parks, the water features in the gardens (nice for running and swimming in if you're Arthur) and there was even a rainforest for Arthur to revisit his youth in if we had time.

And there was another reason to hope we were going to have a good time. The day of our event was also my birthday, and not just any birthday – my fortieth. I thought that if I couldn't spend my special birthday with all my family, at least I would be with Arthur. And there would be some consolation in that we would be spending my birthday evening at our publishers' dinner in the magnificent Dickson Palace, a neo-Renaissance mansion in the middle of Gothenburg. One of the most famous places in the city, it would be quite a way to celebrate.

Happily, Arthur was quite relaxed these days about getting into a kennel ready for a flight; I found I didn't have to worry like I used to about his separation anxiety (although I still, and always will, put one of my T-shirts – smelling of me – into his kennel with him for the flight).

As it wasn't a long flight to G'burg, we arrived at the airport fresh and ready for our next adventure. As if by magic, the first people we spoke to when we came through Arrivals at the airport were a couple who, even as they came towards us, I could tell were fans of Arthur's.

'It's so wonderful to see you,' said the husband as soon as they came within earshot. He and his wife were beaming, and looking so happy to see me and Arthur. 'We've just flown in from Karlstad for the book fair, specially to see you.'

'And now you're here,' said his wife, looking up from patting Arthur's head. 'It's so wonderful what you've done. God bless you for your kindness.'

'Yes,' her husband said, 'you are a lesson in unselfishness. We had to come and meet you.'

They seemed to vanish almost as soon as they'd arrived. Like so many who loved our story, they just seemed to want to meet us and thank us for reviving their faith in human nature. I knew, from all the many, many messages and cards and even phone calls, that people seemed to draw strength from the way in which Arthur and I had fought to be together, and how our sacrifices had led to happiness for both of us.

Many people seemed to take our story and put it into the context of their own lives. I had even had a card from a 93-year-old woman, enclosing a photograph of her leaning on her Zimmer frame. She had taped a picture of me and Arthur onto the front of the frame, as if being reminded of our courage and determination could give *her* courage and determination.

'Hey Arthur,' I said to him, as I bent down to give him a hug, 'it's all good, isn't it? We have each other. And it's all good.'

Saturday dawned. The day of the big event, the big dinner – and my big birthday. The day started very well with a Happy Birthday call from Helena. It was lovely to hear her voice, and then lovely to hear Philippa sing 'Happy Birthday' down the phone. Thor joined in too, but being only a year old, I'm not sure he knew the words as well as his mother and sister.

It carried on being a good day, because Arthur and I went for a run in Slottsskogen Park, a huge wooded recreational area in the centre of the city, perfect for dogs who need a proper run. It was a warm September day, and it was great to see sunshine glinting on the green of the beeches and oaks. Arthur seemed to be in his element. No doubt there were loads of interesting smells to explore, but he also loved the stream that flowed through the middle of it all. Watching him splashing about, just as he did in the lakes at home, I marvelled again at how much he loved the water. Cool Swedish streams and snow, such a world away from the South American jungle, and yet so clearly the world Arthur loved.

We went on to do a signing session on the outskirts of the book fair itself, and then started to make our way towards the venue where we were due to be interviewed, hooking up with Anders, our publisher, along the way. The reaction of the crowds was amazing; at every moment we were surrounded by admirers, all wanting to say hello to Arthur, and to tell us how much they loved our story.

It meant that it took way longer than it should have done to get to the venue – I couldn't not let people say hello to Arthur, since that's what they'd come for, so we let them all have a chance even if it did slow us all up. But eventually we arrived at the venue – a big carpeted area surrounding the table and chairs where the interview was going to happen. I think we must have made quite a spectacle as we arrived. I know we made a lot of noise, because Arthur was still a bit over excited from his run and was barking back when people applauded.

We arrived during the second half of the previous event, which was the famous Alex Schulman, journalist and TV personality, who was talking about his new book. The problem was that when people clapped, Arthur felt he had to join in. So when the audience clapped Alex Schulman they were almost drowned out by Arthur barking. I had a feeling Mr Schulman might not have been amused. (And as it later turned out, I was right. He made a podcast in which he said that dogs don't belong at book fairs.)

Happily unaware of any of this, Arthur and I got ready for the interview. I was glad to see that we had a sold-out event, but a bit less glad that it was starting to feel hotter and hotter. Something to do with a warm day and a lot of people packed in . . .

Anders went off to get some water for Arthur. As he came back carrying a plastic bowl with water slopping about in it, he caught my eye and said, 'I don't usually bring my authors water in a bowl. But I think he'll find this a bit easier than that water glass in the studio the other day.'

It was standing room only at the back, and people crammed in on every available bit of floor at the front. We got a wonderful reception after the talk, and when I thanked everyone for coming I hope they knew how much I meant it – and how much it all meant to me.

Leaving Anders to see to his other authors, we headed off towards the Bonnier stand where we were giving an interview to *Expressen* – the people who had followed our story so closely right from the beginning (as they still do). It was slow work to reach the stand, and after the interview I thought it would be good for Arthur (and me) to have a rest away from the crowds. Not that Arthur seemed in the least bit fazed by the crowds, but if we could get away for a bit of quiet time I might snatch a chance to call Helena and tell her how it had all gone.

The Bonnier stand was huge, as you'd expect from Sweden's biggest publisher, and it had a VIP area on the upper level on top of the stand. Arthur and I headed up the stairs to it. I sat down in the corner and got out my phone. It was then that I became aware of a hissing sound. Uh-oh. All that water that had gone into Arthur just now was coming out. All over the red carpet of the VIP area . . .

I looked around for someone who could help me clear

up. Arthur, who by now had put his leg back down, was looking his most innocent. Even though he was standing next to a huge puddle.

Then from nowhere members of the Bonnier staff appeared with anxious faces and thick cloths. I thought again that it was a good thing everyone liked Arthur so much, as he wasn't exactly your average author . . .

It had been a long day, so Arthur and I went back to the hotel to shower and change. Well, I was going to shower and change; Arthur would just have a snooze. The previous evening, I had left Arthur in the hotel room while I went to a restaurant with Anders and his Bonnier colleagues. But we'd all agreed that there was no way Arthur would be left behind on my birthday, especially as the dinner was in a big private mansion hired by the publishers, so it would be easy to accommodate everyone.

That evening, Anders, Arthur and I arrived at the Dickson Palace dressed in our best (Arthur had his black evening collar on). The place was magnificent. An incredibly imposing building with a huge entrance hall that led into an even more huge dining room. The three of us went to look at the dining room, glittering with the tables all laid up with silver, glass and beautifully written name plates at each place.

I looked at where I was sitting. Right in the middle, next to an author I knew, and surrounded by names I knew from the TV and book worlds. As I went from table to table, I wondered again at the very distinguished company Arthur and I were keeping.

The distinguished company started to arrive, and the entrance hall soon filled up with the buzz of people greeting each other, taking off their coats, laughing and collecting glasses of champagne from seemingly dozens of waiters. It was all most impressive. Arthur stood by my side, not really that impressed, but quiet and happy. Anders introduced us to a couple of fellow authors and then turned to me and said, 'We've got another reason to celebrate tonight, you know. I've just heard from the sales team that *Arthur* has gone straight to number one on the bestseller list.'

'Hey!' I said. 'That's super-fantastic!' I looked down at Arthur, who was still unperturbed by any of this. 'Did you hear that, Arthur? You're number one!'

'It certainly is fantastic,' said Anders, smiling. 'How's that for a birthday present?'

'It's the best,' I said, meaning it.

I went into the dining room, Arthur trotting beside me, feeling great. After all, how often do you get to have a glittering birthday banquet AND be told you are a number-one bestseller?

We all sat down at our tables, and I started talking to the author I knew who was sitting next to me. We all had printed menus in front of us, and I could see that we were in for five courses and every one of them looked absolutely delicious. I'd just put the menu

159

down when I felt a presence on my right-hand side. I looked up. Standing next to me was a formidable-looking lady, glaring down at me.

'I am allergic to dogs,' she said in icy tones. 'It is impossible for me and that dog to be in the same room.'

I gaped. Of all the things that might have gone wrong with that night, I had never imagined this. She was seated on the other side of an enormous room and it seemed amazing that she could be so sensitive to a dog's presence.

Of course, I couldn't say that. I just carried on gaping. Then I said, 'Well, I'm sorry. But I suppose . . . well, I'll have to take him out, then.' The guest continued to glare, and then turned on her heel and stalked off back to the other side of the dining room.

I got up and Arthur, who'd been sitting quietly at my feet, got up too, puzzled perhaps that we were moving so soon. I went over to where Anders was sitting at another table at the other end of the room.

'I'm going to take Arthur out,' I said. 'That lady over there is allergic to dogs. I don't think there's anything else I can do, is there?'

'I'm sorry, Mikael,' said Anders. 'But I'm sure they'll take good care of him in the cloakroom.'

So I went out of the dining room and towards the cloakroom. The girl behind the desk seemed perfectly happy to look after Arthur – who was after all a star in his own right – so I handed over his lead, found a bowl for some water and gave him a big hug. I went back to the table, thinking it was sad that Arthur wasn't at my feet to share this big moment.

Moments later, the first course arrived. It looked just as mouth-watering as it had sounded on the menu. A rich pâté surrounded by delicate salad leaves and four different sorts of toast. Just as I was about to get stuck in, I heard a cough and a hesitant 'Excuse me'. The girl from the cloakroom was standing by my side.

'I think you'd better come,' she said. 'Arthur doesn't seem very happy.'

I got up. I couldn't help remembering the last time I'd been summoned to an Arthur who wasn't very happy. The time I found him howling in despair after that operation when we first got him back from Ecuador. As I walked towards the cloakroom, I could hear him. Nothing like that time in the animal hospital, but a sad sound nonetheless. It was Arthur whimpering and whimpering, and then he'd give a little whine, and then a snuffle. I went into the room at the back of the cloakroom where he was lying. As soon as he saw me he stopped his sad noise. His tail wagging, he came up to me and buried his nose in my hand.

'Hey, Arthur,' I said. 'It's all right.'

The venue manager appeared, with Anders behind her. Arthur was now quiet and subdued.

'If he's not happy here,' said the manager, 'he's very welcome to be in my office – it's just the other side of the hall.'

I looked at Arthur, and the concerned faces around me. I thought of the delicious food that was waiting for me in the dining room. I thought of the feeling of celebration I'd had only moments before. And all on my birthday.

But it was no good. I couldn't eat a five-course banquet and make polite conversation if Arthur was miserable in a cloakroom or an office. Birthday or no birthday.

'Thank you,' I said. 'But it's all right. I think we won't trouble you at all. I'll just head back to the hotel with Arthur.' Anders looked mortified. But what could he do? I knew I was right; I had to leave and take Arthur with me.

'It's all right, Anders,' I said. 'I understand. You can't do anything about it. We'll be fine. See you tomorrow.'

I gathered up my coat and set off into the night. Arthur walked by my side as if we were just going for an unexpected night-time walk. I looked down at him and said, 'If you can't be there, I won't be either. We're in this together; we're a team.'

Heading in the direction of the hotel, we passed a burger bar. The smell of the food made me hungry all over again. But I didn't have the heart – a burger when I could have been having fine steak? I walked on past it and up to the hotel entrance and back to my room. I'd call Helena and get an early night.

Lying on my bed, with Arthur stretched out by my

side, I thought that even if we'd missed out on a great dinner, we had each other. Life was good. I scratched Arthur's ear in his favourite place and said, 'Happy Birthday, me.'

DOG'S NAME: *Dewey*

OWNER: *Emmeline*

FROM: *Humane Society Canada*
and SPCA Montreal, Canada

LIVES: *Montreal, Canada*

'I've fostered and adopted a few dogs in my time, but Dewey will always stand out for me. Sadly he died last year but after a rough start in life we got to have a few great years together, and I can't think of a better dog to be a champion for rescue dogs. I've lived in Montreal for ten years and have been very involved with animal rights during that time, which is how I ended up being a volunteer with the SPCA of Canada during a puppy mill seizure that was undertaken by HS International and the SPCA. All the rescued dogs from the mill had been brought to the SPCA shelter and I was helping to look after them. The dogs were mostly Yorkies, with about ten Chihuahuas, and something about the cheerful, funny, sweet but mischievous nature of the Chihuahuas really appealed to me. Knowing what they'd been through as I did, it seemed amazing to me that they could play so happily in their pens, although it did take them a while to trust new people – especially men.

For the dogs to remain in a healthy condition – physically and psychologically – it was important that they got placed in foster homes after being evaluated. Volunteers like me were a first choice, and I made several choices regarding the dogs with whom I'd connected the most. I felt like I'd bonded most with three Chihuahuas and one Yorkshire Terrier, but ultimately it was up to the employee in charge of placement who she thought would be most in need of a foster home. This is where things took an unexpected turn. Dewey wasn't in the section I volunteered in – he'd been a stud in the puppy mill and had been brought into the vet area because he had health problems due to the poor treatment at the mill. He had severe dental issues and had to have all of his teeth removed. The employee in charge of placements sent me a picture of him when he'd first been brought in and my heart just melted. The next time I was at the shelter I decided to make a pass by the vet area to have a look at him, and I just *knew*. He was the sweetest dog ever. Even now, it makes me cry to remember that moment.

When I first fostered Dewey and brought him home, my biggest concern was how he'd react to my two rescue cats. But I shouldn't have worried – the cats were more curious than he was! He immediately made himself comfy in the bed I'd prepared for him in a big drawer, and stuck his head out to look for me every time he wanted something. He'd been described as 'very shy' on his shelter assessment, and he was, but I soon discovered he was very sweet too. The shyness was the biggest hangover from his difficult past, and he used to tremble when exposed to new situations or environments. He always stuck very close to me, where he felt protected, and he didn't trust other people easily – though I have to say I have a lot of trust in dogs' intuition!

It soon became clear to me that, much as I loved fostering Dewey, I really wanted to adopt him. This wasn't plain sailing, however. I know this might seem unbelievable given the circumstances, but legally the puppy mill still owned all the dogs and the SPCA were locked in a legal battle with them to give up the dogs so they could be adopted. Finally in mid-December 2013 the puppy mill released the dogs and foster families were given priority. I knew by then that I couldn't live without Dewey, so when I heard that I could proceed to adoption I cried tears of joy, and when I got home I hugged him close.

People might not have expected it of a Chihuahua, but Dewey loved the great outdoors and running around. He also got to live in two different countries and enjoyed his stay in both of them: Canada (where he was born) and Ecuador (where I was born). He was such a strong personality, and had no fear of other dogs – even though he was so tiny and looked so vulnerable, he could happily stand next to a Great Dane and make friends. He also loved hiding himself completely under the sheets on the bed, and grabbing sheets and towels and clothes and building little caves for himself, seemingly not even leaving a gap for breathing. If I came and removed a towel when he'd buried himself and left any part of him exposed he would not be happy, so I always put them back. I remember every time I got in from work he would be standing at the door and, as soon as I came in, he would run to sneak himself onto his bed, and wait for me to come and give him attention. It was like a game for him. He fitted perfectly in my purse and came everywhere with me – the supermarket, the shopping centre, and even the cinema and the theatre. He was so adaptable and happy as long as we were together.

Every dog I've had has made my life better, but Dewey is the one who really changed my life. He woke up a maternal instinct in me; I wanted to protect him, and for him to enjoy every minute of life and be confident in every environment. He taught me the importance of caring about the ones we love, no matter how hard life is, and he taught me how to be strong – even though he was so little, he was strong. He'd endured so much, and yet he was so sweet, so loving, and got so much out of life. Because of Dewey I became an even more vocal activist about the puppy mill problem in Canada, and because of him I hope I can make a difference.

Sadly, Dewey was diagnosed with brain cancer in early 2016, and died four months later. I was heartbroken, but he taught me another lesson there – that life should be lived with quality, and that we have to be wise enough, and brave enough, to know when we have to say goodbye. He gave me so many wonderful memories and he was such a wonderful companion. I couldn't have asked for a better dog, and to anyone thinking of getting a dog I would say, 'Please get a rescue dog'. It's a huge commitment, but the love you get in return is pure, unconditional and completely unforgettable.'

DOG'S NAME: *Shakira*

AGE: *6*

OWNERS: *Michelle and Peter*

FROM: *From the streets of Mangalia, Romania. We got her from Föreningen Dog Rescue, which is a Swedish charity.*

LIVES: *Sweden*

'When I moved to Sweden to be with my partner Peter I really wanted to adopt a dog, but I didn't know any Swedish at that point. I Googled for rescue dogs in Sweden but couldn't find any (I now know I Googled all the wrong words). Eventually I ended up on a website for dogs Europe-wide and picked Romania because they had some of the worst stories of how dogs were treated. I found two really large Swedish organisations in Romania and checked out their available dogs via the internet. I searched for a couple of months and then finally found Shakira and fell in love. She was just over a year old when I saw her, and she'd been in the rescue centre for about six months. I showed Peter and he really liked her as well, so we started to talk to the organisation about adopting her.

The woman who had rescued Shakira in Romania, Mihaela, told me that she had been abandoned as a puppy at a petrol station near Mangalia. Shakira seemed to be doing OK so Mihaela had just been feeding her almost every day, until one day she disappeared. An employee at the petrol station told her that their boss had ordered them to take the dog away, and they didn't know where she was. I don't know how long passed but then Mihaela eventually saw Shakira again at a supermarket parking lot. That's when she decided to take her home to her rescue organisation. At the rescue centre they'd assess the dogs' personalities, and apparently Shakira was always the peacemaker between the dogs. We still see that today – if we go to the dog park and a dog is being picked on, she will go and stand up for them.

When the adoption had been agreed and all the paperwork and vaccinations had been sorted, all that was left was to get her home. I remember picking Shakira up from Stockholm Airport. She was so scared. She had never been on that type of slippery flooring before so Peter had to carry her outside as it was making her panic. It must have been exhausting, because she slept for the whole four-hour drive home. Once we got home, she lay down in her bed in the hallway. I sat down with her but Peter said maybe it was a good idea to let her have some time alone to adjust. I reluctantly agreed even though I had never done that with any of my previous dogs. About thirty minutes later I went to refill my drink – only to come back to find Peter lying on the floor next to Shakira, petting her and talking to her gently.

In the early days she was scared of everything, and didn't want to come in the house. Peter had to pick her up and carry her in the first few times. When Peter wasn't around, I had to use meat to entice her inside for about the first week, and it took her about a month before she was comfortable enough to walk around the house. When she slept, she would always sleep with her back against the wall or the couch so she could easily see who was approaching her. And when we went outside, she'd try to run off. She was always happy to meet other dogs but was reluctant to meet other people. She had several other behavioural issues we had to deal with but we were never forceful. We never raised our voices. We just let her take things at her own pace. There were many times we could tell she really wanted to do what we were asking but she was too scared, so we just gave her positive rein-forcement. There is nothing more satisfying than to watch a dog learn to love and trust again.

Five years later, she has completely changed. She's a happy, confident dog who trusts us, and she is comfortable that this is *her* house. We have not tried to walk her without a leash as she's a hunter, but other than that she is perfect. She is the smartest dog I've ever had, and she is also the kindest. When she was in the rescue centre, she lived with male, female, big and small dogs, and she liked all of them. One time, we met a small puppy. The puppy wanted to meet her but was scared at the same time. Without me saying anything, Shakira lay down so she was at the same level as the puppy. It lunged at her face a couple of times, but Shakira just turned her face aside and waited for the puppy to calm down. About a minute later, the puppy stopped lunging, they greeted each other and then started playing.

One of the things I love about Shakira is how hard she works to overcome her fears. When she first saw cows she was absolutely terrified. She would slink by as quietly as she could so they wouldn't notice her, and the minute they looked at her, she would start running. This lasted her entire first summer in Sweden. By the second summer she was OK with them as long as they stayed on the other side of their fence. By the third summer she had got even braver, and this time when they walked up to the fence she cautiously joined them. She even touched noses with one of them. Every day when we walked by she'd look to see if they were around. One day she touched noses with the same cow. This time, the cow licked the entire side of her face. It was definitely a Kodak moment. Shakira's eyes got really big. As soon as the cow was done, she immediately turned and looked at us as if to say: "Did you see that?!"

Shakira has brought so much happiness into our lives, and we hate to think what could have happened to her if Mihaela hadn't rescued her from the streets. If you want a dog, I think it's important to give a homeless one a chance at a great life; a life they deserve. Puppies are fun but it's been my experience that a rescued dog knows what it's like to have nothing or to come from a bad situation. It's hard to describe but their attitude is different. They are much more appreciative of a loving environment. They work hard to be obedient so they don't lose what they have.

It's important to be prepared, though; you have to know about that dog's personality and make sure the dog will fit within the family's lifestyle. Dogs need stimulation and human interaction.

Most importantly, know that dogs have the same feelings as humans. They understand love. They can be happy and sad and they can feel pain just like you or me. But no matter what, they are loyal and will give you unconditional love every day of their life.'

DOG'S NAME: *Smiley*

AGE: *8*

OWNER: *Erica*

FROM: *A municipal pound*
in Romania

LIVES: *Stockholm, Sweden*

'People sometimes ask me why I decided to get a rescue dog and I say, "I didn't – he decided." I was in Romania to do some voluntary work with homeless dogs, but I wasn't thinking about getting a dog myself, and to be honest, I wasn't really in a position to as I didn't have the means or the time. But one day I came across Smiley in the enclosure, curled up behind a kennel and trembling uncontrollably, and something about him reached out to me. I took it upon myself to somehow reach this dog. It took me three days to coax him out of there, and when he finally emerged I had to lift him out of the enclosure because he was too terrified to walk out under his own steam. We tried to get him used to wearing a collar, but it immediately made him roll over onto his back in the 'surrender' position, so we put a harness on him instead. He and I would sit together outside the enclosure, and I would pet him for hours, every day.

One day when I came into the enclosure he abandoned his food bowl, which, when sharing an enclosure with five other dogs, means a definite loss of your dinner to your cohabitants. I realised he had abandoned his bowl to come and greet me, and so he did, with a huge smile on his face. From that point on I couldn't resist him. I knew I couldn't leave him there, as he was deemed too scared to ever get adopted. I was his only chance.

No one really knows Smiley's story. He was scooped off the streets and brought to the municipal enclosure. The municipal enclosures in Romania are way worse than the streets. In this particular enclosure, the dogs lived on bare concrete floors, were fed once a week, and pretty much every single one was terrified of people as they often got kicked. In order to wash out the urine and faeces from the cages, the staff would flush in ice-cold water with a hose. Whether it was summer or winter didn't matter; neither did it matter if the dogs got in the way. This meant that a lot of the dogs had icicles in their fur during winter, and a lot of them starved to death and didn't get any medical attention if they were sick. Smiley was dragged out of there in a noose, scraped against the rough concrete floor.

Bringing Smiley home from Romania was complicated, but the day of his actual homecoming was serene. We stayed at a friend's home out in the forest for the first week, to make the transition into city life a little easier on him. He strolled around while inspecting the cabin, and then he jumped up on the couch next to me, curled up and slept for the whole day, all the while resting his head on my lap. I am convinced that Smiley did once have a home because he wasn't afraid of the floor, the TV or any other indoor paraphernalia like some other rescue dogs, and he was also housebroken.

But he was definitely scarred from his experiences. He was very scared and exhausted, and could only walk for ten minutes before he started panting and falling behind. If the leash ever touched his back he was petrified. He was scared of everything: men, darkness, loud noises, sudden movements, bags, umbrellas, sunglasses, beards, headdresses, crutches, staffs – you name it. The only things I've done to help him are to give him time, encourage him and work hard on building his self-esteem. I never pushed him in difficult situations; instead I've shown him that he is safe with me and that I'm always here with him. Now he's a hundred times better, by which I mean he is only scared of *almost* everything. He's a lot more relaxed and secure and is able to play both indoors and outdoors. He still finds a lot of men very frightening, though, and also loud noises.

Now that he's less scared his personality really shines. He's an extremely happy guy. The people who he is no longer afraid of he really adores. If he meets someone he knows, he will curl his upper lip and show all of his teeth in a huge smile, while prancing wildly. He loves to cuddle, but he has a lot of integrity and it has to be on his terms. Occasionally, if he is already in my bed when I get in, he glares at me, sighs deeply and leaves. Other times he will curl up against me and snore loudly.

He has so many expressions and a great personality. Other dogs don't really interest him, unless they are his best friends, and even then he won't start playing with them until it's already time to leave. I've noticed that he is the most agile and loose-limbed dog I've ever met. If we are out in the forest he will run around for hours, climbing up steep cliffs and crawling under heavy logs. He looks so ecstatic, like he will never follow me inside ever again. He is also very loving when I am ill and can't take any long walks; he is perfectly content with lying next to me on the couch all day.

Having Smiley has changed my life immensely. I've realised that dogs are what is most important to me in life. I went from being a freelancing journalist and tram driver to driving an animal ambulance. I'm also actively working with street dogs, at first in Romania and now in Ireland, and I am working at an animal hospital. My relationships have also changed, and pretty much everything I do now has to do with dogs in one way or another.

Life with Smiley has also ended up being way more interesting, though admittedly not always in good ways! The thing is, if you end up with a dog as scared as Smiley, you will start finding yourself in situations that pre-dog, you wouldn't even have imagined. During his second winter in Sweden, we were out for a walk and Smiley was off the leash for a short time in an area where there were cliffs by the water. Suddenly there was a loud bang and Smiley, a victim of his well-trained defence mechanisms, immediately ran for shelter. The problem was that the shelter of his choice this time was through the fence of a boat club and down into a pit, next to one of the boathouses. There was no way I could get through the same hole, so I sat down outside the fence and tried to coax him out, calling his name. I threw treats in and kept coaxing, but he remained in the pit, frozen, just staring at me.

The gate to the club was locked and the top of the fence was laced with barbed wire. I Googled the name of the boat club in the hope of finding someone to call who could come and open the gate for me, but no one answered on any of the numbers I phoned. I finally panicked and called the fire department. They regretfully told me that they did not have any trucks available, and that they couldn't help me as no one was really in danger. I then simply asked them if I would be reported to the police if I broke in. The fireman asked me how I would do that and I told him I was planning to make my way through the water and climb up on one of the docks to get in. The temperature outside was below freezing and the water was covered with a layer of ice, and the fireman told me that I should under no circumstances put myself in any danger. I stubbornly kept asking if I would be reported, and finally he said that as long as I didn't break anything there shouldn't be a problem. Sorted – so I climbed down to the shore and got in. The water reached halfway up my thighs and with every step I took I felt shards of broken ice grazing my skin through my trousers. I finally reached a dock, pulled myself up and ran towards the boathouses. Smiley was cowering in the pit. I put his leash on and went back the way I had come, wading through the ice-cold water with his 18 kilos curled up on my shoulders. The walk back home was a particularly stiff-legged one, and while Smiley snored on the couch after all the excitement, I ran a hot bath to thaw. The things one does for one's dog . . .

But he really is my everything. The moment when he makes me the happiest is when he comes over, throws his upper body on the floor and looks at me with that wild look and barks at me demandingly. He wants me to let go of everything I'm doing and play with him. It just warms my heart that he has come such a long way from how he was before, that he feels self-confident enough to demand something from me. He's also taught me to relax, and that material things don't really matter, as long as you have a roof over your head and can put food on the table. I would sacrifice everything I have for him.

If anyone was thinking of getting a dog, I'd strongly recommend they adopt. There are so many dogs that need a home, and who could become your best friends. You do have to understand that it's not the same thing as getting a puppy from a kennel or a breeder – you could adopt a dog that has a lot of baggage and acts in ways that you have never dealt with before. But, if you are ready to give the dog all of your patience and the promise of your protection, chances are great that you will get a new soulmate. Like I did.'

Chapter Six

In Sickness and in Health

'It's hard to stop someone who never gives up'

Stockholm, vet clinic, March 2015

This is an awful way to welcome Arthur into Swedish freedom, I thought. Here he is, having put up with four months of quarantine – in a lovely place, but quarantine nonetheless – and four months of our hardly seeing each other. And what do I do? Take him straight to hospital, where he is separated from us once again and given an anaesthetic. It was lucky that I had to spend the hour before he went into the operating theatre giving interviews. If nothing else, it took my mind off the enormity of what he was about to go through.

It was only when I was in the middle of the last radio interview – a 'down the line' interview that I was doing in a side room – that I realised I wasn't the only one who was nervous. One of the nurses was signalling frantically to me to wind up and, as soon as I did, led me back to the waiting room where Arthur had been barking like crazy and running around in circles. As soon as he saw me, though, he calmed down, came over to me and sat at my feet.

I hugged him and comforted him as best I could. But we didn't have long before the vets came in to take him to the operating theatre. It was the beginning of the longest hour and a half I can ever remember. Just as I was thinking it must all be over, and all must be calm, a very anxious-looking vet came into the waiting room. 'You must come,' he said. 'We need you. Now.'

'Me?' I said, thinking this didn't make sense. 'Me? But what can I do?'

'Yes, you,' he said firmly, opening the door for me. I followed him down the passage, where I heard a terrible keening noise, which got louder and louder the closer we came to a door at the end of the corridor.

The vet opened the door. In the small cubicle inside was Arthur, lying in the middle of the room and howling and howling. A noise that was as pained and miserable as any I'd ever heard. I felt terrible. Had I done this to him? My friend, who I was doing everything I could to save and heal?

As I came into the room, Arthur looked round at me. I knelt down and did the only thing I knew how to do. I put my arms round him. In an instant, as if a switch had been flicked, Arthur was calm and silent. Giving a little snuffling sound, he put his head under my arm and I felt him relax. I got down on the floor and lay beside him. After a few moments, I could feel him relax.

We closed our eyes, and stayed like that for a very long time.

Örnsköldsvik, October 2016

It is always lovely to get home after a trip, and coming back from the book tour was no exception. Apart from the slight hiccup of missing the celebration dinner it had all been a great success, and everyone who had a stake in the book was very happy with how it all went. We had also had a bit of a celebration on the Bonnier stand the following day, with everyone coming up to us and congratulating us on our number one. I am not a big one for celebrations, but high-fiving everyone on the stand felt great, and in some ways more like 'us' than any big starry moment could have. Apparently, our book was roaring out of the shops and we were on track to be top of the charts for the next week too.

My priority as soon as we got back was to make sure that Arthur was all right and find out if those lumps were anything to worry about. The rush of activity in Gothenburg had taken my mind off it, but now that I was back so was the worry. Every time I hugged or patted Arthur I would feel to see if the bumps – which I so hoped were just bites – had changed in any way. I was now sure there was another one behind his ear, but Helena assured me that they didn't feel any different from how they'd felt before we'd left. Still, I was very glad we had booked our appointment with the vet for the operation to check them out.

The morning of the operation, I was frightened of making Arthur tense. But I couldn't stop myself doing my usual check of what lumps were where – the ear, his chest, top of his leg. Then, as I gave his nose a comforting pat, I thought I felt a lump there too.

'They did say this sort of thing was common, didn't they?' I said to Helena, tension rising in my voice. 'I mean, lots of dogs have old bites and things like that, is what she said, isn't it?'

'Yes, I'm sure he'll be fine,' said Helena calmly. Although I knew that underneath she was just as concerned as I was.

We got to the vet's ridiculously early, but they ushered us in and took control of Arthur straight away. Helena and I were told to go away and get some breakfast as there was nothing we could do. But we didn't have breakfast, we just sat in the waiting room, trying to distract ourselves by sorting some promotional pictures for the book. Eventually, the door opened. The vet came in smiling reassuringly, and leading a very subdued Arthur behind her. He seemed to be walking as if he were half asleep, or a little bit drunk.

'All went well,' she said. 'We're going to take a look at the lumps we've taken out. The one on his chest was quite big; we had to take a bit more out than we wanted to, just to make sure we had everything.'

I looked at Arthur. He had bandages over his left paw and on his chest and a wound over his nose, and another behind his ear. He looked very battered and a bit dejected, but – I had to keep telling myself – it was for his own good.

'Now he's very sleepy and a bit delicate,' the vet went on, 'so he probably just needs to sleep. He won't want to run around for a day or so.'

Arthur looked up at me. I wanted to think that he understood that I hadn't made this happen to him for a bad reason. I bent down to him, 'OK, Arthur, you're going to be OK,' I said. Arthur looked calmly back at me as if to say he knew, he understood. We went slowly out to the car park. And, yes, of course I lifted him up into the car.

When we got home, Arthur padded softly to one of his favourite places on the floor by the sofa and immediately flopped to the ground. Helena went off to pick up Philippa and Thor from her parents, and I settled down to watch over Arthur.

He seemed so lacklustre, putting his head down on the floor and blinking in a puzzled but stoical way. I had a feeling he felt a bit sick. And, in fact, the sight of the wound on his nose and the bandages on his paws and chest made me feel a bit the same way. When the children got back, they went up to him to hug him gently. Philippa knew that Arthur needed special delicate treatment, of course, but Thor also seemed to know instinctively that he must be careful.

The following day I had to go to the TV studios for an interview on *Malou After Ten* that had been set up before we knew anything might be wrong with Arthur. I had had to tell them it would just be me and, although I knew they were very disappointed not to have Arthur, they were very nice about it.

When I came back from the interview my Instagram was already flooded with worried messages from Arthur's fans. I was glad that so many people cared so much, but somehow the knowledge that other people were worrying only made me worry more.

Arthur was very drowsy for two days, but on the third day he was starting to seem like his proper self again. He had gone out for a little walk with me in the morning, and seemed to be fine – tired when he got back, but basically fine.

And the next day, when Helena was getting ready to take the children for a walk, we were pleased to see Arthur following us around and then standing by the door, which was the place he usually stood when he wanted to make sure that no one was going anywhere without him. When she was ready, Helena opened the door, and out jumped Arthur. His tail was wagging like crazy, and he just seemed to be so happy to be back in action.

Great, we said to each other, happy to see him ready to run about. He jumped up onto the lawn next door and trotted about having a good sniff at every little bit of grass, just as he always used to. When Helena was ready she called out to him. 'Arthur, come,' she said, 'we're all ready now.'

Arthur bounded across the lawn to the wall at its edge, and jumped off. And immediately he howled and howled

– almost like that dreadful keening noise he'd made in the animal hospital that would stay with me for ever.

'Arthur!' Helena said, and rushed over to him. She bent down to try to see what was wrong, and Arthur jumped up at her as if asking for her help. But the jump must have made him hurt even more, because he screamed again. The big wound on his chest, the one they'd had to dig so deep, had opened up and blood was pouring out. 'Arthur, oh no . . .' Helena turned to me. 'You call the emergency vet, and I'll get the children into the car.'

My hands shook as I dialled the number of the animal hospital. They said they were having a very busy morning but of course if we brought Arthur in they would look after him straight away. I lifted Arthur gently into the car. He was now whining in between the little howling noises and he seemed to be bleeding a lot. I rushed round to the driver's seat and we tore off to town and the emergency vet.

They were wonderful – as all the medical people who've ever had anything to do with Arthur have been. Arthur's stitches had burst open when he jumped off the wall, and they had to open up the wound again so that they could set it to heal properly without stitches. The vet explained something about the fact that skin can heal itself inside but the outer layer had come apart. I wasn't following the science of this at all, I was just so relieved that Arthur was all right. He was now so subdued; gone was the happy back-to-normal bounding dog of that morning and now, covered in new bandages, he looked even more battered.

I carried him back to the car, and decided we'd just keep him safe and quiet for as long as it took.

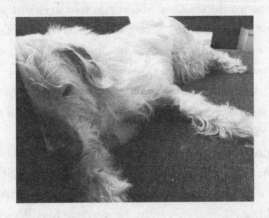

It took over a week. We probably deprived Arthur of some walks and runs that he could have had safely, but I was just too worried about his wounds opening again to take the risk. But eventually we took off the bandages, and went for a gentle walk. Arthur seemed to be a bit slow, and didn't seem to have much energy for all the little extra bits of exploring he usually did. But I came back that day glad that we'd managed a walk all the way to the wood at the top of the hill and back. And that night I went to sleep almost immediately and slept very deeply. All was well with the world if Arthur was on the mend.

A few days later, on a Saturday, I put out some of Arthur's favourite sort of chicken bits. But Arthur just sniffed the food and didn't even give it a lick. He seemed more interested in going outside than having his breakfast. Good, I thought, he's behind on his exercise and he just can't wait to get out there.

I opened the door for him and put him on his long lead, so that he could wander about the two areas of grass at the front of the house. Going back into the house to get ready for a meeting about the hockey team, I called out to Helena who was working upstairs.

'Off soon,' I said. 'Arthur's outside and he seems happy. I should be back for lunch.' I grabbed the keys and headed out of the door.

Arthur was standing on the lawn, quite still, and looking at me. Usually he'd be bounding up to me as if to say, 'Let's get going, we're wasting time here when we could be walking'. I went over to him, scratched his ear and then, when he didn't really respond, knelt down to see if his wounds were still healing up all right. They all looked fine, and I was just about to give him a goodbye pat when my eye was caught by something on the grass.

It was blood. As I bent down to take a closer look Arthur came nearer but didn't go near the blood, as if he knew already what it was and whose it was. I found myself holding my breath. This can only be a sign of something awful, I thought. Surely leaking blood always, always means something terrible is wrong. Now I could see that Arthur's tail had blood on it. There was now no doubt about it – something *was* terribly wrong.

'Helena,' I called out, as calmly as I could. 'I think something's wrong with Arthur. He's pooping blood.'

Helena appeared at the door, Thor in her arms. 'Okaaay,' she said, although everything about her voice told me she knew everything was very much not OK. She came up to look at the blood, and at Arthur.

'Right,' she said. 'You call the emergency vet, I'll get the children ready.' It was as if we now had a well-oiled Arthur Emergency ritual.

The vet sounded calm – properly calm, not our own slightly hysterical false calm – and said if we could be there in ten minutes they'd be ready for us. I lifted Arthur gently into the car and soon the whole family were on the road to the emergency vet.

The vet's offices were next door to a pet shop, which also doubled as a small petting zoo. I'd always thought that was a perfect arrangement, because it meant if small children had to have their pets taken to the vet they could console themselves by playing with other animals.

And I was right about this being a good arrangement – Helena took Philippa and Thor round to the side of the offices, where they could immediately start playing with kittens and puppies. Of course, they knew something was wrong with Arthur, but it was good that they didn't have to sit in a waiting room worrying.

I, on the other hand, had to do exactly that. The vet took Arthur off to an examination room alone. They seemed to be gone for hours. In fact, it was probably only about ten minutes, but to me it felt like yet another long torment of worry and uncertainty in an animal hospital . . .

The door opened. In came the vet with Arthur padding softly behind her.

'I think it must be the painkillers that have upset him,' she said in a calm matter-of-fact tone that took the edge off my panic. 'We can give him something to settle him. But he's not at all interested in food, and that's going to be a problem, I'm afraid.'

I looked at Arthur, who had flopped down on the floor and was half closing his eyes. I could feel myself breathing out with the relief of knowing that whatever was wrong, there was going to be a cure.

'Problem?' I said. 'But isn't there something you can give him to get his appetite back?'

'No, I'm afraid it's not that simple,' she said. 'It's got to be your job. You need to gradually reintroduce him to the idea of water and food. It's going to be a slow process, but it's the only way to get him better.'

And she then explained to me how we would need tiny pipettes to start with, to squeeze drops of water into Arthur's mouth, and then gradually we would use bigger pipettes to drop liquid food into his mouth until eventually he would be able to eat proper dog food again.

I looked at Arthur, now lying on the floor by my chair. He looked as weak and tired as he had that time all those months ago in the jungle, when we gave him all our food and served it to him on a giant leaf.

I had looked at him then, mentally vowing to look after him, 'whatever it takes'.

Nothing had changed.

'Fine,' I said to the vet. 'You tell us exactly what to do, and we'll do it.'

I drove us all home slowly and carefully. Not that I don't normally drive carefully, but this time, knowing that Arthur was in such a bad way, I didn't want anything to happen to upset him, not even a little bump in the road. When we got back Helena got ready to take the children out for a walk. I was going to stay with Arthur and start to practise trying to get him to drink. I got out the smallest dropper that the vet had given us and filled it with water.

Arthur was lying down on his bed, quite still and with his eyes half shut. As I came near he raised his head, looked at me and then – as if the effort had been too much – closed his eyes and dropped his head down again.

'Hey, Arthur,' I said, holding the pipette carefully so it didn't lose any of its contents. 'Hey, boy. Have something to drink. You need something to drink.'

And I carefully lifted up his head, opened his mouth a bit and squeezed eight or ten drops of water into his mouth. I felt better as he seemed to swallow them, and went back to refill the dropper with water.

We had to do this every hour for the first day, and then after three hours start to introduce a little mashed-up food from a larger dropper. And then when Arthur had got a bit more used to that we needed to feed him spoonfuls of food every three or four hours.

I had no idea how long we would be doing this for, but of course we would do everything we could for as long as it took. I was supposed to go to Åre for a meeting in two days' time. I'd wanted to cancel, but Helena told me to try not to worry as she could take over Arthur's feeding easily enough.

We made a special chart that we stuck on the fridge door, with a complete timetable of what Arthur had and when, every hour of the day. One column for water, one for liquid food and then one for when he was ready to have small quantities of solid food. Helena looked at the chart when we'd finished it. 'It's like having a baby, isn't it?' she said. 'He's helpless. And we've got to help him.'

By the time I was supposed to leave for Åre, Arthur was starting to take small spoonfuls of liquid food. But still, I couldn't stand to leave him, even though I totally trusted Helena to take care of him. So in the end I cancelled anyway.

Two days later, Arthur's regime had moved on to his having tiny bits of chicken (his favourite) in between the liquid food. 'I think he's really on the mend,' said Helena as I watched Arthur sleeping on his bed. 'He got up and followed me into the kitchen this morning. Wagging his tail a bit, like he wanted to be up and eating.'

Of course, all Arthur's friends on the internet were asking how he was, and so were the ESPN film people and the publishers. I didn't want to say anything on social media because it was almost like it would have been bad luck to say he was better when he was still not right, and still not back on his food.

At least he only had one bandage now, so he didn't look quite so wounded, and at least all the wounds were healing properly. We were still waiting for the results of the biopsies of the lumps they'd taken out, but after a couple more days we were taking Arthur outside and on little walks. He seemed to come back from those walks with more and more appetite, there'd been no sign at all of any more pooping blood, and he almost seemed to have his old mojo back.

And then we were plunged back into despair and worry. Whenever we or the children approached Arthur he backed off with a little whimper; he almost seemed to run away from us. He was now mostly back on his food, but he seemed to sit and lie awkwardly, and if you put your hand anywhere near his tail he would yelp in a way I hadn't heard before.

'What on earth's going on with him, do you think?' I said to Helena. 'Look, he's just jumping out of the way.' I bent over to pat his back, but Arthur just sidestepped any sort of contact.

'I think it is his tail,' said Helena. 'Look . . .' and she put her hand very, very lightly on the top of Arthur's tail, and he yelped again and trotted away to the other side of the room.

'Well, I don't care if they're getting fed up with us,' I said. 'We're taking him to the vet again. He's obviously in pain. There must be something really wrong.'

We called the now-familiar number, and were told that – thankfully – we could bring Arthur straight in. This time I couldn't lift him into the car, as he wouldn't let me anywhere near him. But he jumped in of his own accord, almost as if he knew this was the way to get help.

Our vet greeted us with a smile. 'Let's take a look at him, then,' she said. 'I think I know what the problem might be.' Once again she took him away to the examination room, but this time she was back quite quickly.

'As I thought,' she said. 'Arthur's got what we call water tail, or limber tail. It's something that happens – well, we don't know quite why it happens but it's usually something to do with being near cold water or sitting somewhere damp. It's made his tail incredibly sensitive, almost like it's broken.'

'So what can we do?' I said. Arthur had been looking so poorly.

'It will heal itself,' said the vet. 'In fact it might just be something to do with his not having had much exercise lately. Arthur should be better once he starts running around again. And, well, wagging his tail!'

Arthur had looked up when he heard his name. I don't know if it was my imagination, but I could swear he was already looking more cheerful.

'And the other good news,' went on the vet, 'is that we've looked at all those lumps, and I can say that none of them are anything to worry about. One of them is just an old tick bite, and everything else is benign.'

I felt such a flood of relief. I realised that for the past few weeks I'd been holding my breath, and that worry about Arthur had been gnawing away at me. Having had so many months of being glad to have him well and happy after all that he had been through, I had scarcely allowed myself to think that we might lose each other now. It was a thought, I realised, that I almost literally couldn't bear. Bending down to give Arthur a (careful) hug, I knew that I would finally sleep well that night.

After that last visit to the vet, Arthur seemed to get better and better until, after a particularly long walk, with him bounding about just like his old self, I thought it was safe to put a message on social media telling everyone that he was officially recovered.

The flood of happy messages that came back made me smile all over again. I felt sure that those oceans of goodwill flowing Arthur's way must have helped him. It was as if he was a living symbol of good things and of hope.

Happily, Arthur was much better by the time we got to the deep winter of Christmas and New Year. And by the time we got to January and all the work I had to do preparing for the major pond hockey tournament in Örnsköldsvik harbour, Arthur was there to help me. It was a huge undertaking – literally lights, camera, action, as well as commentary by two well-known Swedish TV personalities – with hundreds of people to manage, and logistics to be planned. People said it was the highlight of the Örnsköldsvik year, and in the days afterwards I felt such pride – as well as relief – that the whole event had lived up to my own very high expectations. And on the sparkling bright morning afterwards, as I watched my friends take down the arc lights, pack away the spectator stands and box up all the equipment, I clipped on Arthur's lead and we set off for a walk round the harbour. It felt somehow fitting that after such a big event I should have some quiet time with my friend. He trotted along by my side, thankfully now so well and healthy, looking up at me from time to time as if just to make double sure I was still by his side.

The next few weeks saw Arthur getting stronger and stronger, and then he was completely like his old self. Or, at least, the self that he had become with his new family. He bounded about in his beloved snow, played with

Philippa and Thor, wolfed down his food – and all the while keeping his usual watchful eye on me and the rest of his family, just in case he might be missing out on something.

Outside the snow was as thick as ever in all the right places for those who wanted to run about – or ski. We were finding out that Philippa was fast developing a passion for skiing, and it was wonderful to see how quickly she took to it. In fact, she never seemed to want to stop, even when it was almost dark.

One Sunday, we came back from a weekend of skiing to the usual host of emails for me and Helena. In among them was one from ESPN – their documentary about Arthur had been nominated for an Emmy Award for its camerawork. I looked down at Arthur as he lay calmly on his black bed. He certainly looked like an award winner to me, and if he won I knew that he would treat his triumph like he treats everything else, with the cool, calm, collected dignity that had made me notice him all those months ago in Ecuador. There was an email, too, from the book agent, who said that there were producers in Hollywood interested in making a feature film.

Even though he wasn't looking at me, I smiled at Arthur. How wonderful it would be, I thought, if even more people could share in our story, and see that anything is possible if you care for someone enough and are determined enough. And yes, I thought, he'd make a good movie star.

It still seems extraordinary that just a few short years ago neither Arthur nor I knew the other even existed. And yet now it seems as if he has always been there, always made me feel complete.

I have no idea what the future holds. One step at a time. But one thing I do know is that what I said in the documentary, and what I think every day of my life, is true: bringing Arthur into my life is the single best thing that I have ever done. Or am ever likely to do.

Acknowledgements

If someone had told me three years ago that I would have a friend called Arthur and that he was from Ecuador, on the other side of the world, I would never have believed them.

At that time, I was an adventure racer. And that meant that everything was about having the strength and the skill to race well, to compete at the highest level. That was it. I spent every waking hour training and thinking about how to do better.

But on the 14 November 2014, that all changed. Everything changed when this dirty and wounded stray dog walked up to me as I was putting my bike in its box and refuelling for the last stretch of the World Championship race. What happened after that is almost surreal. Who could have imagined that a couple of meatballs could start a lifelong relationship?

The two books about Arthur would never have been written if it hadn't been for **Val Hudson**; I think she is the person who knows me best besides Helena. Val has told my story in a beautiful way. She is a wonderful person with a heart of gold – if you met her you would understand.

Thank you **Philippa** and **Thor**, for everything. Even though the media attention means our lives aren't quite the same as other people's, thank you for being such great kids. You are the bravest!

Helena, you are the knight of the family. Even when the days are full and you are so busy, you still find time to take care of everyone. You are everything I would like to be.

Arthur, you are such a very special individual. I am not saying just 'dog' because that doesn't seem to do justice to you. You are wise, strong and the best family member anyone could imagine. I am the luckiest man on earth to have you as a friend.

Picture acknowledgements

© Michael Bergman: integrated image on page 183

© Krister Göransson: integrated images on pages xi, 3, 40, 48, 52, 77, 82, 90, 95, 98, 113, 147

Colour images in plate section numbers 3, 4, 12, 14, 15

© Kate Hewson: integrated image on page 88

© Marie Jungsand: colour image in plate section number 10

© Helena Lindnord: integrated images on pages 41, 119, 149

Colour images in plate section numbers 5, 11

© Mikael Lindnord: integrated images on pages xii, 5, 75, 81, 123, 145, 155, 189, 197, 200

Colour images in plate section numbers 1, 2, 6, 7,9

© Thom McCallum: colour image in plate section number 13

© Håkan Nordström: integrated image on page 44

© Ale Socci: integrated image on page 17

© Magnus Stenman: integrated image on page 181

Colour image in plate section number 8

Every reasonable effort has been made to contact the copyright holders, but if there are any errors of omissions, John Murray Press will be pleased to insert the appropriate acknowledgement in any subsequent printing of this publication.

Mikael Lindnord made his name as an adventure racer and race planner. As a boy he wanted to be an ice hockey player, but failing to make a professional team at the age of 17 set him on a different path. After doing military service he became an adventure racer and travelled the world competing in the AR World Series. Now retired from competitive racing, he is a motivational speaker, event organizer and is back playing hockey again. He is also involved with the forthcoming movie that will tell the story of how he and Arthur found each other and fought to be together.

Arthur is from somewhere in Ecuador. He may be made up of many breeds, or he may be an Italian hunting dog. He likes walking, running and relaxing with Mikael and his family in Sweden.

As an editor of non-fiction at major publishing houses, **Val Hudson** published many ground-breaking bestsellers. Now a full-time writer, she is the author of a wide range of non-fiction and, as Chloe Bennet, the 'Boy Watching' series of novels for young teens.

Read where the story began …

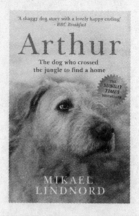

When you are racing 435 miles through the jungles and mountains of South America, the last thing you need is a stray dog tagging along. But that's exactly what happened to Mikael Lindnord, captain of a Swedish adventure racing team, when he threw a scruffy but dignified mongrel a meatball one evening.

When they left the next day, the dog followed.

Try as they might, they couldn't lose him – and soon Mikael realised he didn't want to. Crossing rivers, battling illness and injury, and struggling through some of the toughest terrain on the planet, the team and the dog walked together towards the finish line, where Mikael decided he would save Arthur and bring him back to his family in Sweden, whatever it took.

ARTHUR: The dog who crossed the jungle to find a home. Available now.